Barry Norman is ... ular film critic. He be... nter of the BBC *Film* p... *Film '72*; by the time ... ome a household na... ther documentaries and programmes, including *Tonight* and *Omnibus*. In the late 1970s and 1980s he wrote and presented four acclaimed series on *The Hollywood Greats* and one on *The British Greats*, and the ten-part BBC series *Talking Pictures*, all of which were backed up by bestselling books.

Barry started his writing career as a journalist on the *Kensington News* and was Show Business Editor of the *Daily Mail* until 1971. He has contributed over the years to the *Guardian* as occasional leader writer and Wednesday columnist, to the *Observer* as sports writer, to *The Times* as television critic, and also as a scriptwriter for the cartoon strip *Flook* in the *Daily Mail*. Barry has also written many novels and works of non-fiction, including books on film and cricket.

www.transworldbooks.co.uk

BARRY NORMAN

See you in the Morning

BLACK SWAN

TRANSWORLD PUBLISHERS
61–63 Uxbridge Road, London W5 5SA
A Random House Group Company
www.transworldbooks.co.uk

SEE YOU IN THE MORNING
A BLACK SWAN BOOK: 9781784163426

First published in Great Britain
in 2013 by Doubleday
an imprint of Transworld Publishers
Black Swan edition published 2014

Addresses for Random House Group Ltd companies outside the UK
can be found at: www.randomhouse.co.uk
The Random House Group Ltd Reg. No. 954009

Penguin Random House is committed to a sustainable future for
our business, our readers and our planet. This book is made from
Forest Stewardship Council® certified paper.

Printed and bound in Great Britain by Clays Ltd, St Ives plc

2 4 6 8 10 9 7 5 3 1

This book is for our families, Diana's and mine, because we both felt that family was the most important thing in life.

Contents

Preface

'TWO WEEKS AGO I lost my wife and the best friend a man could ever hope for.'

That was the first line of a piece I wrote for the *Daily Mail* on 12 February 2011. You may well wonder what I was doing writing for a popular newspaper at a time when my wife, Diana, had just died and the overwhelming emotion for me and mine was grief. I have two explanations: the first is that if you are a writer (and I've earned my living by writing ever since I left school) your immediate reaction when something either wonderful or, in this case, truly awful happens is to put it all down on paper. It's sort of cathartic. Writing about the death of Diana (known to those closest to her as Dee) did nothing to assuage the sense of grief or loss – I feel them still – but it did at least help me to express and crystallize those feelings.

When I first wrote the piece I had no intention of offering it for publication. It was just for me. But then – and this is my second explanation – on re-reading it, I realized how very special Dee was. She was beautiful, highly gifted, mildly eccentric, always wonderful company, loving and greatly loved. And then I decided I wanted other people to know these things – not just the many devoted admirers of her novels, but everyone.

So I wrote to my agent, Gordon Wise, asking if he thought any newspaper would be interested in my jottings. The *Mail* responded eagerly and wanted more, and I was happy to give them more, just as I was happy a year or so later to write this book. Dee is still a huge presence in our lives – mine, our daughters', our grandsons' and that of her surviving brother, Tony. She was irreplaceable and we talk about her all the time, very possibly to the intense boredom of our friends.

She was simply a wonderful person to know and my hope is that some inkling of that comes across in the following pages.

Incidentally, the title – which at her request is also inscribed on her tombstone – is part of the mantra we exchanged every night: 'Love you. Sleep well. See you in the morning.' It was a kind of superstition, I suppose; we felt that if we didn't say those words something dreadful might happen during the night.

It worked for fifty-three years, three months, two weeks and a day. And then, alas, it didn't.

1

A Night at the Circus

GOD, HOW MEMORY plays tricks. For decades, memory has been telling me that I first met Diana early in 1957; Wikipedia now tells me I'm wrong, that it must have been late in 1956, because that's when the Moscow State Circus first came to London. Well, okay, Wikipedia is often no more reliable than the memories of those who contribute to it, but this time I think it must be right because Charlie Chaplin's penultimate film, *A King in New York*, was released in 1957 and, given the amount of time it takes to make a movie, he can't have made it in the same year so . . .

Right then – 1956. A Sunday evening. Autumn, winter? Whatever. A damp, dark evening, anyway, and the Moscow State Circus had just arrived in London. Oh yeah, big deal, you might think, and so it was then.

London in the mid-fifties was still in the grip of post-war austerity, and exotic foreign entertainment was hard to come by. The Moscow Circus was not only foreign and exotic but world famous, and all the national newspapers had sent reporters, me included, along to record its arrival.

I was twenty-three, a gossip writer on the *Daily Sketch*. I mention this apologetically rather than boastfully, because gossip writing is not a trade to boast about. I used to excuse myself by saying it was the only job in newspapers I could get at that time and at my age, but that wasn't true. In fact, I'd been offered jobs as a reporter on two much more respectable newspapers than the *Sketch* – the *Derby Evening Telegraph* and the *Scottish Daily Mail*, as well as the Press Association in London – but had turned them down in favour of the *Sketch* for two reasons: one, I didn't want to work anonymously for a news agency; and two, I'd fallen in love (or thought I had) with a secretary at Ealing Film Studios and was desperately eager not to leave London.

Not that it did me much good. The desirable secretary, a little older and much more worldly than I, had recently broken up with her boyfriend because he was rather given to knocking her about. But within a couple of months of my starting to take her out she went back to him and unceremoniously dumped me. What is it with some women that they're attracted to men who treat them badly rather than gentle ex-public schoolboys like me? Go figure.

So I was stuck with a job for which I had little taste or aptitude on a newspaper which nobody really liked, and not even a girlfriend to show for it.

The *Sketch* then was a bit like the *Sun* is today, only not so outrageous; it dealt in innuendo rather than blunt, screw-and-tell exposure of the sexually in-discreet, because newspaper editors at that time were much more frightened of the laws of libel and contempt of court than they are nowadays. Even so, it was pretty mucky and also parsimonious. It took me on as a 'trainee' gossip writer because that way it could pay me only £12 a week, which was some way below the union minimum.

However, there I was on that Sunday night, young, raw, a bit out of my depth at, I think, the then Harringay Arena as the circus people started putting up their equipment. I didn't know any of the other journalists, who, unlike me, were news reporters rather than gossip writers, and they were all more experienced and older than I was – all, that is, except one: a slim, fair-haired, very pretty girl about my age, who moved comfortably and with easy familiarity among them. The others all obviously knew and liked her, in marked contrast to what seemed their obvious reluctance even to be introduced to me.

How we got to talking I don't recall. Maybe she felt

sorry for me, standing alone on the fringe of the crowd, or maybe we were simply drawn towards each other because we were clearly the youngest people there.

We introduced ourselves. 'Diana Narracott of the *Daily Herald*,' she said, offering a firm handshake.

'Barry Norman of the *Daily Sketch*, actually the, er, Simon Ward column, the diary, you know,' I replied.

'Oh,' she said.

I used to get that kind of cool response – or worse – quite often. Once, I turned up, uninvited, to a birthday party for Stirling Moss, possibly the best racing driver never to have won the world championship, and announced myself to the birthday boy.

'Oh, Christ,' he said, 'is there nowhere you can go to get away from the bloody Simon Ward Diary?'

Similarly, a peer of the realm when asked by me why he thought his wife had run away with the master of the local foxhounds merely replied: 'What bloody business is it of yours?' and slammed the door in my face. I couldn't blame him; I'd have done the same in his place.

Diana, though, was more polite than that, though clearly disapproving of my trade. (In an interview many years later she said she had thought it 'very infra dig' and, frankly, she wasn't wrong.) Unlike me, she, as I came to learn when asking colleagues about her, was a highly respected reporter; indeed, at twenty, she had been the youngest reporter in Fleet Street.

On the night of the circus she was charming and

friendly, although not as friendly as I, already a touch smitten, would have liked. Later, much later, she was to confide in friends and, I think, our daughters that she, too, was a little smitten, but she gave no indication of it. Not for a moment did she even hint that if I were to call her at her office she wouldn't immediately slam the phone down, and I was far too gauche and unself-confident around women to suggest that perhaps we might, but only if she really felt like it, of course, meet again some time.

So we parted, and that, I thought regretfully, was that. Our paths had never crossed before and, given that her job concerned hard news and mine dealt with tittle-tattle, there seemed no reason why they should ever cross again.

I couldn't get her out of my mind, though.

Next day in the pub – the White Swan, aka the Mucky Duck, where journalists from the *Daily Mail* and the *Sketch* did their working-hours drinking – I happened to mention to my colleague Tom Merrin that I'd met a girl called Diana Narracott the previous night. Tom, it turned out, was an old friend of hers; both of them had worked a few years back for the same group of local papers in the East End of London.

'Oh, yeah,' said Tom, when I mentioned her name. 'That Diana Narracott. I wouldn't mind getting my leg across her.'

Personally, I like to think I would have put it rather

more delicately, but I could certainly sympathize with his ambition. Still, that was Tom for you – a product of the East End, tough-looking though actually kind and gentle but given to telling it like it was. I asked what he knew about her, knowing that if there was any insalubrious gossip he would have passed it on, but, to my relief, he had only good things to say about her, although why that should have concerned me is hard to tell since I never expected to see her again.

Tuesday passed uneventfully and on Wednesday morning I was sent to St Margaret's, Westminster, to cover a wedding. St Margaret's is a very posh church hard by the Abbey, where, by and large, the weddings involve only toffs and their upper-class totty. I forget which toff and totty were tying the knot that day and, anyway, it doesn't matter: for me, the only important thing was that, amazingly, Diana was there, way off her usual hard-news beat and not looking happy about it.

She held gossip columns and their contributors in mild contempt and here she was surrounded by gossip writers, which might have been bad news for her but was exceptionally good news for me because I was the only gossip writer she actually knew. So she came to sit beside me in the back pews to which the press had naturally been relegated, because none of the invited guests would have wanted to be seen sitting with journalists. Well, you never know what you might catch from the creatures.

Once again, she was charming and friendly, but no

more. Once again, I was too shy to suggest that we might, you know, meet again, on a sort of date, like, if that was okay with her. So, once more, when the wedding was over, we went our separate ways to our respective offices, mutually mumbling that it had 'been good to see you again'.

On the Friday of that week, Charlie Chaplin held a press conference at Shepperton Film Studios to announce production of his next film, *A King in New York*. With my movie connections – Dad being a noted film producer and director – I was chosen as the one to cover this event. So, in mid-afternoon, I drove to Shepperton in my Morris Minor, a car that had taken me from Johannesburg to Salisbury (now Harare) in Southern Rhodesia (now Zimbabwe) and, several months later, from Salisbury to Cape Town.

I cannot recall a word Chaplin said that day or even what he was like, for, to my astonishment, there among all the news reporters and showbiz and gossip writers was Diana yet again. This time we greeted each other like old friends, and when the conference was over and we had all written our stories and dictated them to our respective newspapers, I asked her how she was getting back to town.

On the coach with most of the others, she said, because she had no car of her own. Indeed, in the mid-fifties, very few people had cars. Now this was my chance, and I took it.

'I'll give you a lift if you like,' I said.

'You have your own car?'

'Yeah.'

'Wow!' she said, and I felt that this was the first time I had really impressed her.

As it happened, she wasn't going back to central London but to Paddington Station, where she was to catch a train to Torquay. She had the weekend off and was going to visit her mother and two younger brothers at the home she was buying for them in Plainmoor.

Paddington was a bit out of my way but, what the hell, if she'd asked me to drive her to Torquay I would probably have done it.

On the way, we found out important stuff about each other. I had no girlfriend; she had no boyfriend. I lived with my parents in Edgware, Middlesex; she shared a flat in Wanstead, East London, with her friend Trixie Neuburger, a secretary on the *Sunday Mirror*. We both wanted to write novels.

And we both marvelled at the fact that though she had been in Fleet Street for more than three years and I for nearly eighteen months we had never previously met, and yet, in less than a week, we had been thrown together three times. It must, we agreed, be Fate, and therefore it would be a very good idea if we went out together the following week. Indeed, we were both so enthusiastic about this that before she got out of the car at Paddington Station we sealed the agreement with a kiss.

I watched her as she walked towards the ticket office, thinking, 'Boy, did you get lucky!' and 'Roll on next week!' and little suspecting – because, like most people, even professional fortune-tellers, I'm rubbish at predicting the future – that this fascinating young woman was to be the most important part of my life for more than fifty years.

2

Someone Like Diana

O UR FIRST DATE was hardly a huge success. In fact, it was a non-event. On the Thursday after she returned from her weekend in Torquay, we had arranged to meet for dinner at the Trocadero, Piccadilly, which was then a smart but fairly in-expensive restaurant. Today it's a kind of entertainment complex with a cinema, arcade games, places to eat, and now, unlike then, a bit downmarket.

Expense was important. I was then on about £18 a week, and Diana was probably earning up to half as much again. But though I was living at home and my parents didn't charge me rent, I had very little money to spare and she even less. She was, after all, paying half the rent on the flat in Wanstead and the full mortgage on the house in Plainmoor. Church mice, certainly any who might have a financial portfolio, were probably better off than she was. Her outfits were always neat and carefully, though conservatively, chosen, but just a little well-worn; new clothes, unless something positively had to be replaced, were clearly a luxury she couldn't afford.

But, never mind, dinner at the Troc, though somewhat out of my league had I been eating alone, was something I felt I could run to. If push came to shove, I might even be able to charge it to the *Sketch* as expenses.

As it happened, though, the dinner never came about. At the last minute, Alan Gardner, the editor of the Simon Ward Diary, found an event – some sort of tedious debutante party – that apparently only I could cover that evening, and there could be no argument.

Alan was always doing that kind of thing. One Sunday night, I was about to leave the office when he said: 'You live in Edgware, don't you?'

'Yes,' I said.

'Oh, good. On your way home could you just call in at Blackbushe Airport? Deborah Kerr's flying in from somewhere or other at nine o'clock and it might make a good paragraph.'

Now, Edgware is in Middlesex; Blackbushe Airport was to hell and gone in the opposite direction on the Hampshire–Surrey border. I tried to explain this, but Alan was unconvinced. 'Oh, it's just a small detour,' he said, and that was that. I eventually got home at about two o'clock in the morning.

In those days, if you worked in Fleet Street the job came first. Always. If you felt it didn't, then you yourself would no longer have a job. Simple as that. Maybe the same applies now with circulations declining as people increasingly get their information from the Internet and newspapers cut back on staff. But then, especially at the *Sketch*, it was a reign of terror: do as you're told or get out.

Of course, newspapers and journalists have changed dramatically over the years. The papers themselves are more gossipy and sometimes more spiteful, broadsheets are now the exception rather than the rule and a newspaper's website is increasingly important, often attracting more readers than the printed pages.

The practice of journalism itself has altered a lot, too. In my day, there was a heavy drinking culture; we gathered a great deal of our information during on- and off-the-record interviews over long, often rather boozy, lunches, and our working hours were extremely elastic. It was not unusual to turn up at the office one morning, be sent on an assignment and not get home for several days. Probably the latter is still true, but today's journalists certainly don't drink as much as we did. Indeed, it sometimes seems to me that, except for the likes of parliamentary reporters and lobbyists, they don't even get out much. They appear to do a lot of their work hunched over their computers and lunch off a bottle of designer water and a sandwich from Marks and Spencer or Tesco.

However, on the day of our first proposed date, I called Diana to tell her that the evening was off, convinced that such an abrupt let-down could only mean the relationship was over before it had even begun.

But, thank God, she understood. She, too, knew what it was to be putting your coat on preparatory to leaving the office after a hard day's work only for some executive to say: 'Oh, by the way, on your way home could you just...?' thereby blowing whatever imminent social engagement you had in mind clean out of the water.

What happened on her twenty-first birthday is a good example. At that time, the twenty-first, not the eighteenth, birthday was the big one, the day you came of age and joined the grown-ups. Diana was working the day she became twenty-one and was looking forward to an evening of celebration with her colleagues in the Cross Keys, the pub opposite the *Herald* building, but as she was getting ready the news editor summoned her. There'd been a murder in Southampton and she was to go and cover it.

'But it's my birthday,' she protested. 'My twenty-first!'

'Many happy returns,' said the news editor. 'Now bugger off to Southampton.' And she did, and her birthday was celebrated in her absence.

So her understanding was crucial on that night of the date that never was. Every previous girlfriend I'd ever had would, if stood up at the last minute on a first date, have let it be known in the coolest possible terms that henceforth we would be strangers. They'd have believed that I didn't care or that I'd found a better prospect, but they weren't fellow journalists and Diana was.

Eventually, though, we did meet, and kept on meeting, and I found myself acquiring a reputation in Fleet Street, not because I was a particularly good journalist – I wasn't then, though I like to think I got a lot better later – but because I was Diana Narracott's boyfriend. In those days, Fleet Street was, as it had been pre-war, very much a boys' club; female editors or executives (except on the women's pages) were unheard of, and even female reporters, especially very attractive young ones, were a rarity, and Diana was much lusted after. Not only when she was on an assignment with reporters from other papers but even in her own office she found herself constantly rebuffing advances from middle-aged men who, either because of their seniority or because they'd fought in the war or both, felt they had some kind of *droit du seigneur* over her. To all these old lechers, along with people of much my own age, I was an object of envy.

After that first momentous week I don't think we ever met again on an assignment, but we met frequently in the evenings and then went off together by car. At that time, parking in London wasn't all that difficult either during the day or at night. There were no meters and no traffic wardens. You simply drove around for a few minutes until you found a convenient space and parked. Then you left your car there as long as you wanted. And it was free. Hard to believe now.

So I would collect Diana outside the *Daily Herald* office and we'd either have a couple of drinks with her colleagues in the Cross Keys or go for a meal and then I'd drive her home to Wanstead. I didn't know then and I don't know now how far that is, but it seemed a bloody long way. Certainly, it was well after midnight before I got home, but I didn't care. Very soon I realized that, as far as I was concerned, and, I hoped, as far as she was, too, this was serious, although ours was a pretty chaste romance.

This is the fifties I'm talking about, when nice girls didn't and nice chaps didn't ask them to. It wasn't like the sexually liberated sixties when, apparently, even on a first date it was a question of your place or mine, whereafter it was clothes off and into bed. No, no, in the fifties female virginity – though not of course male, perish the thought – was still a much-prized commodity. Nice girls and nice boys had to be well on the way to the altar before anything more than heavy petting came into consideration.

But be that as it may, it wasn't very long before I took

Diana home to Edgware and introduced her to my parents.

They both liked her immediately; so did my brother, Rick, and sister, Valerie. And one evening my mother took me to one side and said: 'When you get married, son, I hope you marry someone like Diana.'

I didn't realize then that when she said 'someone like Diana' she meant precisely that, not necessarily Diana herself, because, after our marriage, their relationship was pretty fraught for several years. I don't think Mum ever really believed that any girl was quite good enough for her sons, nor any man good enough for her daughter. Ideally, she would probably have liked us all to remain single and living at home. So, after our marriage, Mum's affection for Diana turned to suspicion that she wasn't looking after me properly, and maybe something even worse than that.

Diana was still working for the *Daily Herald*, still being sent abroad on assignments where quite often she was the only woman among a group of male reporters, and Mum could never come to terms with this. It was a generation thing. In her view, a married woman shouldn't be gallivanting around Europe with a bunch of blokes. The fact that it was common in journalism, that the women, like the men, were there to work and tended to come home in the same state as they left wasn't easy for her to grasp. Oddly enough, she didn't show the same concern when I was one of the blokes surrounding a lone woman. Maybe she felt it was different for men.

Actually, the first intimation I had that Mum might have suspected Diana of infidelity came years later, when our elder daughter, Samantha, was born. The first thing my mother did was to look at Samantha's hands. When I extend my hands, the fingers tend to curl upwards quite noticeably. It was a characteristic that we three children shared with Dad. So Mum took hold of Samantha's hands and stretched them out and, phew! the fingers curled upwards.

'That's a relief,' said Diana. 'I think she's pretty sure now that you're the father.'

3

Crossing Continents

RIGHT – NOW WHERE did it all begin? I was born in London on 21 August 1933; Diana – actually Mary Diana, though she never used her first name – also in London, four days later. She delighted in those four days; every year after we were married she would, between 21 and 24 August, tell anyone who cared to listen that she was married to a man a year older than herself.

My parents, Leslie Norman and Elizabeth (Betty) née Crafford, both came from poverty in South London, both left their London elementary schools at the age of fourteen, both trained in Wardour Street, the London headquarters of the movie industry, to be film editors, and both worked in the thirties at the British Independent Pictures studio in Elstree, although my mother gave this up after I was born.

They'd been married in 1930, when Dad was only nineteen and Mum three years older. Rather differently from Diana, she used this age difference to address my father as 'Son', usually with affection but sometimes ironically.

By the beginning of the Second World War, Dad was reckoned to be just about the best film editor in Britain, but then the army summoned him. Many of his contemporaries in the movie business, largely Oxbridge-educated (for the film industry was very much a middle-class occupation in those days), somehow managed to avoid this fate, possibly being better connected than he was, and advanced their careers nicely during the war years.

Dad, however, was conscripted to help develop sonic warfare, which entailed making the noise of large troop movements to fool enemy forces into attacking the area the sounds were coming from, thus enabling the British army to creep up behind them and take them by surprise. It was an ingenious idea and sort of worked, although the only time Dad put it into practice in the Burmese jungle he did it so effectively that the Japanese army, which our lads were trying to creep up on, said (though not, I suppose, in quite these words): 'Christ, that's a fucking big army over there!' and scarpered in the opposite direction. As a result, when the British troops turned up, all they found was Dad and his sound crew. Just as well, too, because if the Japanese had got there first they would certainly have killed him and his men.

By the time the war ended, Dad had risen to the rank of major (a title he immediately discarded on returning to civilian life on the grounds that to continue using it would be too pretentious). Michael (later Sir Michael) Balcon, head of Ealing Studios, used his own connections to get him demobbed early in order to edit *The Overlanders*, the story based on fact of an Australian rancher who drove his cattle across the country, at a time when a Japanese invasion seemed imminent, to save them from falling into enemy hands. It was directed by Harry Watt, a brilliant documentary maker who then had little experience of feature films, with the result that, although much of the material was superb, the overall film was a mess, and foiled the attempts of every editor at Ealing to knock it into shape.

My father, recommended to Balcon by Charles Frend, the director for whom Dad later produced *The Cruel Sea*, took a unit to places like Kew Gardens to film necessary linking shots and did such a good job of editing that the picture was a great success. So he was swiftly signed up by Balcon and, after editing *Freda* and *Nicholas Nickleby*, went on to produce films such as *Where No Vultures Fly*, *West of Zanzibar*, *Eureka Stockade*, *Mandy* and *The Cruel Sea* before directing the likes of *The Night My Number Came Up*, *Dunkirk*,

The Shiralee and *The Long and the Short and the Tall*.

For me, my brother Richard or Rick (born 1938), and our sister Valerie (born 1946), ours was a comfortable middle-class existence, although we could have been a lot more than comfortable if Dad had not been so cautious in financial matters. Our mother, though virtually uneducated, was a very shrewd businesswoman; at one time she owned a wool shop in Edgware and did nicely out of it. But what she really wanted to do was buy flats and houses to rent out. On my father's salary, which, though by no means abundant, was way above the average wage, this would have been quite possible, but he had no faith in property as an investment. In the forties and fifties house prices hardly changed and he saw no reason to believe they ever would. So he vetoed Mum's scheme, which was a real shame, because she had a good eye for a house and a bargain, and I reckon that if she'd been given her head my parents would have ended up pretty rich.

Diana's childhood circumstances were rather different. Her parents were Arthur Narracott, a journalist later to become the Air (originally the more grandly titled Aeronautical) Correspondent of the London *Times*, and Aeron Franklin, a trained nurse. In the late thirties and into the early war years Diana and her parents lived with Arthur's uncle, the Rt. Hon. Ernest Brown, who at various times was Minister of Labour and National Service, Secretary of State for Scotland

31

and Minister of Health in Churchill's coalition cabinet, and was apparently possessed of a very loud voice. It's said that, once, during the war when walking along a corridor in the House of Commons, Churchill heard shouting emanating from around the corner.

'Who's that?' he said.

'Oh,' said his companion, 'that's Ernest Brown talking to his constituents in Rugby.'

'Well, can't he use the bloody telephone?' said Churchill.

We (before the war, anyway) had one maid; the Browns, who had a large house in Camden Town, had several – 'my servants', as a diminutive Diana once grandly described them and was immediately so contrite that forever after she blushed with shame when she recalled that moment.

But when the Blitz started Aeron decided London was no place for her daughter and took her to live in Torquay. Arthur, by now a war correspondent for *The Times*, stayed put, and that really was the end of the marriage because he met somebody else, asked for a divorce and remarried.

Torquay was Aeron's destination of choice partly because it was a long way from the London Blitz and partly because that was where her parents lived. No big house and no servants awaited them there, though initially Aeron did rent a house where she, having trained and worked as a nurse, established a day nursery. But that came to an end when a bomb dropped in the back garden. Nobody was hurt but apparently the blast caused the back door to turn all the way round so that a raincoat hanging on a hook started off inside the house and ended up outside, still on its hook. With the place now uninhabitable, mother and daughter moved in with Aeron's parents, who had a flat above a shop in the middle of the town. This was not a particularly happy time for them. Diana's grandfather, the chief engineer at Torquay's Imperial Hotel, then one of the finest in the land, was affectionate and good-natured, but her grandmother was an irascible, hard-drinking Welsh woman, much given to betting on the wrong horses and of unpredictable temper.

But there was nothing else for it. Aeron, now working as an assistant in a chemist shop, could not afford a place of her own, especially when Diana's brothers, Tony and Roger, came along, so there they all stayed until Diana was able to buy them the little house in Plainmoor.

Unlike me, who never had a part-time job – not even a paper round – Diana had to work in her school holidays, in a flower shop or tearooms. Once, when her employer asked her to stay late, he offered her by way of recompense 'a day off in lieu'. Diana was close to tears. 'But I don't want to spend a day off in Looe,' she said. 'I don't know anybody there.' Well, she was very young.

When she was fifteen she left school and worked on

a local newspaper, before moving to East London, where she lived with Aeron's sister Peggy and her husband, Alfred Jermyn, and their family. For a while she had a job as a reporter on an engineering magazine, though what she didn't know about engineering could have filled Wembley Stadium. She left that job when an editor chased her round the office with carnal intent. Oddly enough, I later worked with that same editor on the *Daily Sketch*; he wasn't an editor there, just an unpleasant, deeply lascivious little bloke who eventually went to prison for beating a girl with a coat hanger in a fit of sexual frenzy. By coincidence, another guy I worked with there got into some trouble for a sexual offence, rape in his case. I don't know; maybe there was something in the air at the *Sketch*. But, if so, I'm happy to say it didn't infect me.

After leaving the engineering magazine Diana joined one of a chain of local newspapers in the East End before being recruited at the precocious age of twenty by the *Daily Herald*.

Meanwhile, I'd left school at seventeen, although my teachers at Highgate School wanted me to go to Cambridge. I could have done that; my A levels were easily good enough and it wasn't difficult for public schoolboys to get into Oxbridge in those days. But, stupidly perhaps, I decided my education had already cost my parents enough money and it was time I supported myself. I had a long chat with my father one afternoon in the garden during which it was decided that my first choice of employment – a job in the cutting rooms at Ealing Studios – was unwise. Dad could easily have wangled it for me and even got me a union ticket (absolutely essential at that time), but the British film industry was in one of its many periods of slump – a lot of qualified technicians were unemployed and there was no guarantee that I, as a mere trainee, could hold a job for long.

So I opted for my second choice, journalism. I've never regretted it. If I'd gone into the film industry I'd have been carrying too much baggage; people would have said, 'He's only here because of his father . . . Not nearly as good as his father . . . Must be a great disappointment to his father.' In newspapers, where Dad had no influence, I had to stand or fall by my own efforts and abilities.

My first job, aged just eighteen, was on the *Kensington News*, a weekly now defunct, where I stayed for fourteen months. At the end of that time I realized that every day I was covering exactly the same events as I had on the same day the previous year. Not good enough; I needed more varied experience if I was to progress, but it seemed there wasn't a paper in the land prepared to take on a nineteen-year-old with fourteen months in the job.

Happily, I was in correspondence with Ron and Sylvia Elliott, who were family friends. Ron, in his mid-thirties, had worked as an accountant at Ealing Studios, and one summer I'd turned out alongside him, as a guest player, for the studio cricket team. Now he and Sylvia had moved to Johannesburg, where Ron worked for a film company. I told him of the professional stalemate in which I found myself, he put me in touch with Argus South African Newspapers and they offered me a job on the munificent salary of £9 a week on the *Star*, an evening paper in Johannesburg. It was a lot better than the £3 15s I was earning at the *Kensington News*. So I accepted and, on 6 March 1953, the day after Josef Stalin and Sergei Prokofiev died, I sailed to South Africa, where I lodged with Ron and Sylvia for the best part of two years, by which time I had become heartily sick of apartheid.

Since I wasn't brave enough to stay and try to fight the political system put in place by the Nationalist Party and the racist Afrikaners who supported it, I thought at first of going home. Then I decided that since I was there I'd better see a bit more of southern Africa and arranged a transfer within the Argus group to the *Rhodesia Herald*, a morning paper in Salisbury. There I lived in a flat rented from a colleague, who himself had transferred within the Argus group to Ndola, and stayed for seven months before setting off on a drive from Salisbury, via Beitbridge, down to Johannesburg and thence to Cape Town and a ship home.

What now surprises me is that at no time during that

long drive did I feel remotely in danger, except briefly when my car was surrounded by a disgruntled family of baboons while I was crossing the semi-desert region of the Karoo. Indeed, as a reporter on the *Star*, I had often found myself wandering around downtown Johannesburg at two o'clock in the morning without ever feeling at all threatened unless I happened to come across a bunch of hairy-arsed Afrikaners, who hated everyone English as a matter of principle. Certainly, any Africans I met were harmless, largely because they – unlike me and the other blankes (whites) – had to have passes to be there in the first place.

But, forty years later, the BBC Radio 4 programme *Sentimental Journey*, which invited people to return to places that had been important to them in their youth, took me back to Jo'burg and, God, what a difference. By then, apartheid had gone, but in its place was an atmosphere of brooding menace. We – Arthur Smith, the comedian who hosted the programme, the production team and I – were warned never to walk around the city alone after dark; it was just too dangerous. And as for driving alone to Cape Town, I wouldn't have contemplated it unless I was heavily armed. It's great that the Africans are finally in control of their own country but deplorable that the white minority governments that had previously ruled them had never prepared or educated them for such responsibility. The infinitely wise Nelson Mandela, with his policy of reconciliation, did his best to make the handover of power as smooth and non-violent as possible, but, alas, it didn't take with everybody. Certainly, it had precious little influence in Zimbabwe, where President Mugabe has pursued a policy of persecuting the whites while, at the same time, systematically trashing his own country.

When I lived as a young man in both those countries each was a white man's paradise; the blacks were your servants, never your equals. In both countries, particularly Southern Rhodesia, if you wanted a black girl in your bed that was fine, so long as you didn't make it too public. In neither place was it remotely acceptable for a white woman to take a black man to bed. In Salisbury it was not uncommon to see a white man walking hand in hand with a black girl, though admittedly never a black man with a white girl; in Johannesburg in either case they would both have been arrested, prosecuted and very possibly beaten up in the cells. In South Africa there was an Afrikaans word *voertsek* (literally, 'away, say I'), which was used offensively to dismiss troublesome dogs and Africans, or kaffirs, as they were contemptuously known. I don't imagine a white man would dare use it to an African now, and quite right, too, but I wouldn't want to live in either country again.

So in the early summer of 1955 I left southern Africa, came home, joined the *Daily Sketch* and, of course, met Diana.

4

In Sickness and in Health

IPROPOSED TO DIANA in her flat at Wanstead one
evening after we'd been out to dinner. The full works
– me on bended knee before her – and she said yes.
Quite enthusiastically, too.

And so to the wedding arrangements. They weren't
easy. Traditionally, of course, the father of the bride
footed the bill, though I'm not sure that tradition still
applies. But not in our case, and for various reasons. In
the first place, Diana's parents, Aeron and Arthur
Narracott, were long divorced and, besides,
Arthur rarely saw Diana, his only child. Once, she
phoned him at his office, saying cheerily: 'Hello, Daddy.'

'Who's that?' said Arthur, suspiciously.

So the chances of him coughing up for the wedding
were pretty remote. (Actually, I rather liked him. We
only met a few times, but we got along well, as

journalists tend to, having the same kind of anecdotes and experiences to exchange. Besides, he had played cricket for Devon and cricket is one of my great passions.)

With Arthur reluctant to have anything to do with it and Aeron much too poor even to contemplate picking up the bill, there was only one option left – my parents would arrange matters. In fact, Mum had wanted to from the start and went about the job with great enthusiasm. At that time, any doubts she might have had about Diana's suitability to be my wife either had not yet sprung up or were well hidden, because she seemed happy about the marriage.

The wedding was fixed for 12 October 1957 at St Margaret's church, Edgware, and a huge marquee was erected in our back garden for the reception.

The guest list was a bit complicated because Diana seemed to be inviting everyone she met, so we were never quite sure how many to cater for.

And then, about a week before the event, she got the flu. One day when I went to see her she was feverish and burbling about 'seeing little people', elves and fairies and the like. I reported this back to Aeron. 'Oh, God,' said Aeron. 'She hasn't invited them to the wedding, has she?'

On the day itself Diana was on the way to recovery although not completely there. Arthur turned up to give her away and when she joined me at the altar and we knelt together, she said somewhat irritably: 'You'll have to hold on to me. I'm likely to collapse any minute.' Not a great start.

The reception went well, though. Quite a few of Diana's friends had travelled up from Torquay, and Dad had invited Richard (later, of course, Lord) Attenborough and his wife, Sheila Sim, along with Donald Sinden and his wife, Dinah. My father had, as producer, worked with Sheila on the film *West of Zanzibar* and with Donald on *The Cruel Sea*. The following year he was to direct Dickie in *Dunkirk*. So they were all pretty good friends and, indeed, in our wedding album there's a picture of Dickie kissing Diana while Donald kisses the back of Dickie's head and Sheila, Dinah and I look on. That must have been one of the rare occasions when, for a moment, it was the bridegroom who felt like the spare whatsit at his own wedding.

The honeymoon, arranged through an agency that dealt with members of the National Union of Journalists and the civil service union, was to be in Porto Cristo, Majorca. The charter airline we were flying with had a coach terminus at Marble Arch, where all the passengers were to gather, thence to be taken to Blackbushe Airport.

Dad elected to drive us to Marble Arch. A seriously bad idea because, like everyone else, he'd been at the champagne. In fact, he nearly killed us about ten minutes after we set out when he veered on to the wrong side of the road and only just averted a head-on crash with a lorry coming the other way.

Diana had been very eager that the other people on the charter flight shouldn't know we were on our honeymoon. 'I don't want anyone oohing and aahing all over us,' she said.

Fat chance of escaping that. In the first place, her going-away outfit included a fluffy pink hat and a pale blue suit. She looked gorgeous – exactly like a young woman embarking on her honeymoon. In addition to that, in the party that escorted us to Marble Arch was her matron of honour, Trixie Neuburger, still obviously dressed for a wedding and with some kind of wreath tipped jauntily over one ear. Along with her was one of the ushers, in full morning suit. John, his name was, a portly young man with spectacles, a friend of Diana's family who, at one time or another, had proposed to both her and her mother and been courteously turned down on each occasion. He was extremely drunk and kept putting money in the coffee machine, then lifting the resulting coffee carefully towards his mouth before tipping it all down his shirtfront. He did this, I think, three times.

Anyway, we looked like a circus, eliciting mirth and shouts of 'Congratulations!' about equally.

The rest of the night was even worse. When we got to Blackbushe we found the airfield smothered in fog.

Nothing was coming in; nothing was going out. So Diana and I spent the first night of our marriage dozing and leaning against each other while we sat upright on a green leather bench.

Once we arrived, however, the honeymoon lived up to all our expectations. True, we were woken about six o'clock every morning by building works across the street, which was not exactly ideal for a couple who hadn't necessarily gone to sleep early. But the hotel, though simple, was adequate and the flight and full board for two weeks cost us only £37.50 each. We teamed up with two other, slightly older and longer-married, couples, one from Morecambe, the other from Scotland. The Morecambe couple, Roland and Joan Bett, became long-time friends. The six of us used to go to a local bodega in the evenings where everything except champagne cost 2d a glass – and I'm talking old, pre-decimalization, pence here, which is probably too small even to convert into modern currency. Champagne, or strictly speaking cava, admittedly was a lot more expensive, running to half a crown (12½ pence) a bottle. One night we went to a nightclub where I grandly forked out another 12½ pence for five champagne cocktails and a glass of Madeira. Always a big spender, me.

But honeymoons come to an end and we returned to reality, to a rented flat in Highgate, big and dark and full of heavy Victorian furniture. Marriage probably doesn't come as any kind of culture shock to people nowadays when couples often live together before getting hitched. But we hadn't done that; neither of us had ever lived with anyone of the opposite sex so the business of adjusting our behaviour and customs to fit in with those of someone else was entirely new to us. Neither of us really knew what to do. Diana was used to fending for herself; I was not. I'd either lived at home, where my mother provided my evening meals and, on Sundays when I wasn't working, brought me a full English breakfast in bed, or I'd lived in South Africa and Rhodesia, where servants did all the cooking.

It was now that I discovered Diana couldn't cook, or rather that she could cook two, and only two, dishes – cauliflower cheese and shepherd's pie. Her favourite was then and remained cauliflower cheese, which I've always disliked, but her shepherd's pie was okay. So, since I was incapable of cooking anything, those were the two dishes we lived on for what seemed like months while we grew to dislike each other quite intensely for several reasons. The flat was gloomy and uncomfortable; we had very little money; we both worked long hours and spent little time alone together, and we were both family-ridden. She was devoted to her mother and to Tony, her adopted brother, and her half-brother, Roger (the son of an American serviceman, who went off to D-Day and was never heard from again).

Aeron had acquired Tony early in the war. A friend of

hers, whose husband was with the army in Europe, had become pregnant by a Polish officer. (Diana always claimed that Tony's father later left the army, found religion and became Pope John Paul II, but, trust me, there's precious little evidence of that.)

The woman was, naturally, desperate. She loved her husband and didn't want to lose him. As was no doubt the case with countless women during the war, her affair with the Pole had been no more than a fling, inspired by loneliness as much as anything else. What to do? When her husband came home she could hardly present him with a baby and try to persuade him that it was the result of a gestation period lasting a couple of years. So she turned to Aeron, who was then still running her day nursery. Would she take the baby? Aeron said she would. The woman went away to give birth, secretly, in another part of the country and when she returned Aeron met her at the railway station and was presented with Tony, a pram and a ten-pound note. And that was it. They parted, and Aeron went home to introduce Diana to her new brother.

And, in every important sense, a full brother is precisely what he became, as did Roger a year or so later. They didn't all share the same bloodline, but that never mattered to any of them. They were a family and a very close one.

Yet it could have been so different. Early in the war Aeron, by now divorced from Arthur and long before

Tony and Roger came along, was engaged to Kenneth Farnes, the former Essex and England fast bowler, who was a pilot in the RAF and did his training in Canada. On the night of 20 October 1941, soon after he had returned to the UK, Aeron was waiting for him at an airfield where he was due to land after a night-flying exercise. He never made it. Exactly what happened is unknown, but he was killed when his plane crashed near Chipping Warden in Oxfordshire.

With Farnes dead, Aeron never did marry again. But by the time I got to know her she had long assembled her very happy, though decidedly offbeat, family – both boys had different surnames from hers: Lennard in Tony's case, Franklin in Roger's – and Diana insisted on visiting them as often as she could.

I resented that, just as she resented my frequent trips to my parental home in Edgware.

On top of that, I was a lousy husband. Diana would hurry back from work to prepare an evening meal – cauliflower cheese one day, shepherd's pie the next – while I would hang out with the lads in the Mucky Duck, returning home in the middle of the evening to find the dinner either spoiled or, in her case, already eaten.

And so it went on. After a few months we decided this wasn't good enough for either of us and that the best thing was to separate. She even went home to Devon to tell Aeron. 'This marriage isn't working,' she said. 'I'm going to leave him.'

'No, you're not,' said Aeron. 'You're going back to make it work.' I don't know why she said that because in those early years I was often quite unpleasant to Aeron – surly and resentful – but when it came to possible marital bust-ups between her daughter and myself she was always on my side, or at least on the side of the marriage, for which I am eternally grateful. Maybe she saw something better in me than I presented to the world.

Apart from Aeron, though, what really stopped us parting was the thought that if we threw in the towel after only a few months we'd look stupid in the eyes of our friends. And in addition to that, as Diana said, we'd have to return all the wedding presents and we no longer had any idea who had given us what.

So we decided to give it a year for appearances' sake and stayed together. Reluctantly.

I've always thought, and for a long time believed we both did, that that first year of our marriage was incomparably the worst. But later on Diana was to tell other people that the second year was just as bad. I don't remember that; my feeling is that once we'd left Highgate and moved into a more modern, two-bedroom flat above a butcher's shop at Fiveways Corner in Hendon things started to get better between us.

Not that it began too well. Soon after we moved in I was off work for a week with a bad chest infection, then returned to the office too soon and was sent to cover an evening function at the Mansion House. It was

November and bloody cold. I got home very late to find Diana in bed with flu and a raging temperature. We had no doctor, not having been in Hendon long enough to register with one, and we had no phone – many people didn't in those days, especially in furnished flats – so I knocked on the neighbours' doors to ask if they had a phone and, if so, whether I could use it to summon a doctor. Either they didn't or I couldn't. People were, and still are, like that in London and the nearer suburbs; strangers, especially those asking favours, were to be regarded with deep suspicion.

Eventually, I went out to the nearest phone box, about a quarter of a mile away, and called my mother for the number of the man who had been our family doctor since I was a child. He couldn't come and tend to Diana because we were out of his region but he did give me the numbers of other doctors closer to where we lived. I forget how often that freezing night I trudged to and from the phone box, stupidly wearing no overcoat, simply a long-tailed evening suit hired from Moss Bros, before a doctor finally arrived to take care of Diana. Then I went to bed.

The next morning I woke up feeling terrible. That made two of us, because Diana was still feeling terrible, too. I think I must already have been slightly delirious because, despite my wife's illness, I was intent on going to work and returning the hired suit to Moss Bros. I tended to her as best I could and then, because it was still early and I was feeling very cold, thought I might just have a little lie-down before going to the office.

I went into the spare bedroom, found my overcoat and put it over the blankets, got into bed and fell into a coma. Diana, still very feverish, was completely unaware of this. She probably didn't even know I was still at home.

How this might have turned out, were it not for my mother, is anyone's guess. Quite possibly I could have died there and so could Diana, because none of the neighbours bothered to knock and find out how we were. Fortunately, Mum, worried about Diana's condition, drove round to check on her, discovered me in my comatose state and called the doctor. He promptly summoned an ambulance and I was whisked away to the nearest hospital with pneumonia, while Mum wrapped Diana up warmly and took her home to Edgware to recuperate.

I was in hospital for about a week. In those days National Health hospitals could afford to look after patients until they were fully recovered; the practice, which later became common, of kicking them out in the middle of the night as soon as they could walk unaided had not yet been adopted.

One of my first recollections when I came out of my coma was not auspicious. I heard an old man in the next bed die. I'd seen the nurses wheel him in, his weeping wife beside him, slide him on to the bed and pull the curtains around him. Then they went away and for a while all I could hear was the wife sobbing. But suddenly there was this strange, harsh, throaty sound, followed by the woman's scream. I'd never really believed in the death rattle before, but I did now.

Meanwhile, Diana was recovering comfortably in Edgware and getting on well with my family, though there was one nasty moment when she'd been playing chess with Rick and, having lost, threw his chess set on the fire. Well, she never was a good loser. Once, when we were living in Highgate, we had ten shillings (50 pence) between us to last the whole weekend. Fortunately, we had enough food in, but we obviously couldn't go out anywhere so we spent the two days either reading or playing cribbage. She was pretty good at crib but on this occasion the luck wasn't with her and I beat her six times in a row, whereupon she hurled a hairbrush at me with a memorable cry of: 'You can take so much but this is a straw!' She was always getting commonplace phrases wrong. Once of a man she disliked she said: 'He's a nasty cup of tea.'

When I came out of hospital we both stayed for a while in Edgware, then returned to Hendon, and Diana went back to work. I, though, was off for six weeks before the doctor said I could return to the office, so I must have been pretty ill.

5

A Hack's Life

SOME MONTHS BEFORE all that happened I had left the *Daily Sketch*, where I had become editor of the Simon Ward column, and joined the *Daily Mail*. I resigned from the *Sketch* because the paper's editor, Herbert Gunn, had on appointing me promised me a rise after a few months but, when I reminded him of this, launched a sneering attack on the column in his daily bulletin. This bulletin, consisting of his often spiteful views on that day's paper, was posted on a board in the newsroom for everyone to read. Previously, the gossip column had hardly got a mention but now it came under quite savage attack almost every day. When this had been going on for a week or so Gunn called me to his office and announced triumphantly that since he obviously had such a low regard for what I was doing he couldn't possibly give me a rise. He didn't divest me of my job; he just refused to give me any more money. I thought, Bugger that, and handed in my notice.

I wasn't unemployed for long. Alan Gardner, my predecessor as editor of Simon Ward, had earlier joined the *Mail* himself to edit their gossip column, the Paul Tanfield Diary, and he recommended me to the news editor Donald Todhunter as a promising news reporter. I spent six rather pleasant weeks news reporting before the extent of Alan's Machiavellian plotting became apparent and I found myself transferred – whether I liked it or not; and I didn't – to the Tanfield column as Alan's deputy. He knew I disliked gossip writing but he thought I was rather good at it, so having me beside him was what he had planned all along. Back to square one then, though on a much better newspaper. Until the seventies, when it merged with the *Sketch* and went tabloid, the *Mail* was taken seriously as one of the 'quality' papers, along with *The Times*, the *Guardian*, the *Daily Telegraph*, the *Financial Times* and – hard though it is to credit nowadays – the *Daily Express*.

As time goes by, the years and the events tend to blur together and it becomes difficult to remember exactly who did what and when. But I do recall that while I was doing vitally important work, such as interviewing well-heeled, well-connected debutantes at their coming-out balls, Diana was flitting around Europe, reporting on the Queen's official visit to somewhere or other, following Princess Margaret around Belgium, returning home to go on a military exercise with the Royal Marines Commandos (cunningly disguised as one of them) and, for a few momentous days, pursuing the former British and Commonwealth heavyweight champion Don Cockell as he chased his errant wife and her lover to Spain. Irene Cockell had suddenly upped sticks, taken the family car and caravan and run off with a merchant seaman named Johnny Clark, whom she had known for only six weeks but with whom, she said, she had experienced love at first sight.

Cockell, the nation's press – Diana among them – in close attendance, had tracked them down to Sevenoaks, where he confronted Clark, and an unseemly and in-determinate brawl ensued, before the runaways took off for Spain, the wronged husband and a mob of journalists panting at their heels. It all ended sort of happily, because Cockell and wife were reunited, though only briefly. But what Diana always remem-bered most vividly about this incident was that at one point the runaways and Cockell literally took flight in different planes. So did the pursuing journalists, and Diana, who had hitched a lift on the *Daily Mirror*'s rented aircraft, found herself shouting: 'Follow that plane!'

Meanwhile – for I don't wish you to think I wasn't leading an exciting life, too – I had an experience of my own with Princess Margaret. She had gone to a circus and I was covering this momentous event for the *Sketch*. During the performance a trapeze artist or tightrope walker (one or the other) had fallen from his equipment and landed in a bit of a heap on the ground below. Since he got up and walked away I thought this rather clumsy of him and not worthy of mention in my report. My fellow hacks, however, took a different view. The next morning, according to their newspapers, it appeared that the princess had been overcome with horror as the unfortunate bloke hurtled to the floor before her very eyes and barely escaped death. My recollection – the accurate one, I assure you – was that, like the rest of us, she had gasped a bit when he fell and then, again like the rest of us, had laughed in nervous relief as he staggered away.

I told Gunn this when he summoned me to explain how I had been so comprehensively scooped, but he wasn't impressed. Never mind whether my version was closer to the truth: the lesson clearly to be learned from this was that you should never let the facts get in the way of a good story. Since this was something I refused to take on board, I never could understand why Alan Gardner had such confidence in me; I was a crap gossip writer.

There was one other occasion that Diana always remembered with great fondness. The year 1959 was declared World Refugee Year, and Fleet Street seized upon this with enthusiasm. Early in the year a mock refugee camp was set up under the radio mast at Crystal Palace and a bunch of journalists went to live there for a week to show their readers how tough it was to be a refugee. I wasn't among them – gossip writers weren't invited – but Diana was. Years later, in his autobiography *In My Wildest Dreams*, the bestselling novelist Leslie Thomas remembered the event like this:

> There was only one woman, Diana Norman, the pretty wife of Barry Norman the television presenter. She collected our shillings and went out into the outside world to purchase vegetables for our nightly cauldron of stew. She also did our sewing and organized the household tasks. By the end of the week there was not a man there who was not hopelessly in love with her. She handled the situation especially well and returned to her husband quite unperturbed by these devotions . . . Our mutually felt regard for Diana was such that we became over-protective. She slept amongst us in our hut. No one embarrassed her and if they had I swear the others would have fallen upon him like dogs. Once a visitor to the camp . . . smiled a little too much at her and we stood in a rough group and growled at him.

Well, that was Diana; throughout her life she was a one-woman charm offensive. Lots of men fell in love with her. Why she stuck with me I will never know, but I'm eternally grateful that she did.

As for Les Thomas, he was an old friend of us both; he was working for the *London Evening News* when Diana was with the *Daily Herald* and I was with the *Sketch* and the *Mail*. He is one of the great successes of the Dr Barnardo's homes – an orphan who went on to success, fame and no doubt wealth. I can still remember an occasion in the early sixties when he and I boarded a bus in Fleet Street, en route to our various assignments, and he told me with understandable excitement that his first autobiography, *This Time Next Week*, had just been accepted by a publisher.

'They're talking about it,' he said, 'as another *Cider with Rosie*.' Well, *Cider with Rosie*, Laurie Lee's account of his childhood soon after the First World War, had been a huge bestseller, something of a minor classic, and I thought Les, or anyway his publisher, was coming on a bit strong. Truth to tell, I was also kind of jealous because I hadn't written anything but newspaper articles yet, though I desperately wanted to. Anyway, I was totally wrong. *This Time Next Week* was a big success and Les's first novel *The Virgin Soldiers* an even bigger one.

On reflection, it was a strange life we led at the start of our marriage, Diana and I. Sometimes, as she pointed out, I would be flying into the country (for I, too, had my occasional trips abroad) while she was flying out. That sort of thing being fairly common, it's not surprising that marriages between journalists, particularly young journalists, so often fail, and it could well have been another reason why our first year together was so unhappy and unsettled. We loved each other, I'm sure of that, but we didn't really know each other because we didn't have enough time together for that.

During those early years Diana and I both had encounters with long-time heroes, each notable only for the fact that it happened. Hers was with Raymond Chandler, creator of Philip Marlowe and daddy of all crime writers. He had long been an idol for both of us, and one evening when she was with a bunch of other journalists in the Savoy Hotel in London she spotted him morosely propping up the bar. By then he was widowed, by all accounts inconsolable at the loss of his wife and near the end of his own life. Diana and the other hacks were there on a different assignment, and she was the only one to approach him, not for the purposes of an interview – though that would have been welcome – but simply so that she would ever afterwards be able to boast that she had met Raymond Chandler.

It wasn't a successful meeting. She said he was polite but uninterested in anything much except the drink on the bar in front of him. They chatted for a few minutes and then she left him alone, departing with the impression of a sad man who had pretty well given up on life.

I think it was this experience that led her to the conclusion that perhaps it's best not to meet your heroes, because so often they fail to live up to expectations. When you think about it, there's no reason why they should. The hero or heroine is not responsible for the expectations; they're entirely yours and he or she has no obligation to conform to them.

Maybe that's why Diana adamantly refused to meet actors she admired, although there were exceptions, Laurence Olivier notable among them. I got to know him very well in the early sixties when he was founding the National Theatre at the Old Vic, and one night I took Diana along to a small drinks party at his flat in London. She, like me, already admired him enormously as the best actor either of us was ever likely to see on a stage, and now she fell for him completely. He, like her, had the ability to charm anyone when he set his mind to it. Charm is a great gift but a somewhat dubious one; anyone who has it can use it ruthlessly, turning it on or off at whim. I've seen both Diana and Larry do that. Anyway, she fell for him partly because he was very nice to me and she tended to base her opinion of anyone famous on whether he or she treated me well. She disliked Alistair MacLean, the bestselling author of *HMS Ulysses* and various other novels, intensely because she was convinced he had insulted me at a dinner party at the Dorchester Hotel. If he had, I either didn't notice it or chose to ignore it, because I'd known Alistair for a while and got along with him pretty well. Besides, he was drunk that evening, as he often was in the latter part of his life. I tried to explain this to Diana on the way home, offering the booze taken as an excuse for any real or presumed slight, but she was unconvinced. 'He was rude to you,' she said, 'and I'm not having it.' Thereafter it was best not to mention Alistair's name around our house.

The evening with Olivier ended up somewhat awkwardly. Diana, who had driven us to his flat, had left the keys inside the car, so when it was time to go home we couldn't get into it. Olivier made helpful remarks about how it was possible to break into a car by using a wire coat hanger and offered to lend us one. But since he had little – indeed, no – personal experience of stealing cars, he couldn't really explain, and neither could anyone else, precisely how the coat hanger should be used. So we called the AA – the motoring lot, not the alcoholic lot – who had the car open in a trice, and we exited, stage left, looking rather shamefaced.

Another exception to Diana's 'for God's sake don't meet the stars' rule was Jodie Foster. Throughout my time talking about films on television I avoided movie premieres whenever I possibly could; Diana avoided them practically all the time. She was much more a theatre than a film person, unless the film had a happy ending, as in the Michael Powell/Emeric Pressburger production *I Know Where I'm Going*, which was her all-time favourite. Movie chit-chat bored her; so did actors of either gender when met face to face. My own reason for giving these festive film occasions a miss whenever I could was the luvvie-duvvie, showbizzy, self- and mutual-congratulation element that reared up. I regard myself as a writer and journalist first, a television presenter second and a showbiz person nowhere. There are many actors and actresses I like, some of them a lot, a few I'm quite glad to have met and others I'd be happy never to meet again. The people I welcomed meeting were not the stars but the directors, producers and writers, who tend to have a much broader, more intelligent and less self-absorbed overview not only of their own industry but of the world around it. I mentioned this once to Michael Parkinson, who said: 'Oh no, the stars, the performers, are the ones I love.' Well, *à chacun son goût.*

Anyway, there was one film premiere in the nineties which I was obliged to attend, and I persuaded a protesting Diana to come with me. I forget what the film was, but at the supper afterwards we found ourselves sitting alongside Jodie Foster, not only a fine actress but also a graduate of Yale, fluent in French and possessed of a very high IQ. I don't think Diana knew much about her, probably not having seen any of her films, but to our relief – particularly my wife's – Foster didn't want to talk just about films but about everything, and Diana was enchanted by her.

Much the same with Kenneth Branagh. In 1996, I was invited to a preview at the Curzon Cinema in Mayfair of *Hamlet*, in which Branagh starred and which he also directed. Diana came with me. We both enjoyed the film a great deal and thus went on to the reception afterwards at the Dorchester Hotel. If we, or especially I, had disliked the picture we'd have gone home immediately, because I could never do that hypocritical stuff of falsely congratulating someone who had made a piece of rubbish with claps on the back and ambiguous declarations like, 'What can I say? You've done it again!' or 'Only you could have made that movie.' Branagh, of course, was there, and I told Diana I was going to talk to him. 'Come with me,' I said. 'I'll introduce you.' Branagh was one of her big favourites, but she refused to go. 'Oh, no, I couldn't. I don't want to meet him.' But I knew she did really; she was just afraid that he would disappoint her. So instead of her going to him, I took him to her and, inevitably, she was charmed.

Branagh shares with Richard Attenborough the aggravation of being sneeringly dubbed a 'luvvie' by tabloid hacks. In neither case is the label remotely justified. Attenborough, admittedly, does call people 'love' or 'darling' but, as he once told me: 'That's only because I can never remember anybody's bloody name, darling' – the final 'darling' there suggesting strongly to me that at that moment he couldn't remember my name either. Both men have contributed hugely to

British cinema and theatre and, in my experience, both are tough, modest and down to earth. The first time I met Branagh was when he came into my studio at the BBC to be interviewed about his latest film. A day or so prior to the event he phoned my production team. 'Look,' he said, 'Barry and I don't know each other. Do you think he'd mind if I came in to have lunch with him on the day? That way, by the time we get to the studio we won't be total strangers any more.'

Would I mind? Of course not. I only wish other actors of his stature had done a similar thing. It makes proceedings so much smoother if interviewer and interviewee have struck up some kind of rapport beforehand. So Branagh came in early and he and I queued up together for coffee and sandwiches in the canteen and, I like to think, have got along very well ever since.

My own encounter with a hero came in the early sixties in Le Touquet, whither I had been dispatched by the Paul Tanfield Diary to cover some sort of grand festival that was going on there. The *Mail* had decided to send a man named Charles Graves with me, he being something of a toff, who, presumably unlike a horny-handed son of toil such as me, could be trusted to find his way around the upper social echelons of Le Touquet and its visitors and, more importantly, introduce me to them.

He was in his sixties, a journalist and writer of

numerous books, many of which fell into the category that Evelyn Waugh once described insultingly – though not with reference to Graves – as 'the history of boot polish'. I didn't like him much. He was patronizing, thought I was a bit of a yob because I didn't hold the stem of my wine glass between thumb and forefinger, and he had an equally posh wife, of about his own age, who had clearly been a flapper in the twenties and still did the flapper thing of droppin' the final 'g' off words like *eatin'* and *talkin'*.

Still, Graves and I found a way to get along without irritating each other too much, and one night we were in the casino, where the most notable person I had spotted was Lord Bob Boothby, the bisexual Tory politician, who was widely believed to have been the lover of Harold Macmillan's wife, Lady Dorothy, and who was in Le Touquet with a young boyfriend. I had a few words with Boothby, but didn't mention the boyfriend in my report; I don't think homosexuality was even legal then. Suddenly Graves said: 'Oh God, there's my brother.'

'Who?'

'My brother. Robert.'

I said, incredulously: 'Your brother Robert? Robert Graves? *The* Robert Graves?'

'Yes,' he said, with a weary sigh, '*the* Robert Graves. Come on, I'll introduce you.'

I was thrilled. I've never been star-struck by actors

(except, just a bit, by Olivier) and reserve any awe I might feel for great sportsmen and writers, the latter because, as a writer myself, I know how damn difficult a trade it is. Of all the then living writers, Robert Graves was my particular hero. I loved his tales of ancient Rome in *I, Claudius* and *Claudius the God*. Indeed, it was reading them that had sent me off in search of works by Suetonius, Tacitus and Plutarch. But most of all I admired Graves's early autobiography, *Goodbye to All That*, which is the finest book I've ever read about the First World War.

So I met him. He was four years older than his brother (who was clearly jealous of him), a burly man, as I recall, with a mop of curly white hair and the face of a Roman emperor himself. I met him and we talked and – well, I did say the only significant thing about these encounters was the encounter itself – I cannot remember a word he said. But, like Diana with Chandler, I can at least say that I met Robert Graves and, when I told her, she was so envious she could have spat.

6

New Arrivals

WHAT SAVED OUR marriage was buying a house of our own in the Hertfordshire village of Datchworth. Before we moved there we'd shifted from Hendon to a disgusting rented flat in Victoria. At a cursory glance – which, alas, is all we gave it before we took it on – it looked fine, but once we'd moved in we realized how truly awful it was. For a start, the kitchen was indescribably filthy, the stove and oven encrusted with grease that might well have had its origin at the turn of the century. You'd probably have needed a pickaxe to get rid of it. Diana and I didn't have the heart to try. In the months we were there we only ever used the kitchen to boil a kettle (for tea) and a saucepan (for boiled eggs).

On top of that, the bedroom faced on to Victoria Street, and we soon discovered that if, when we went out, we left the bedroom window only slightly open we would return to find the bedclothes covered with grit and dust sent up by the traffic passing outside.

The fact that our next-door neighbour was a tiresome young man who showed a fervent interest in Diana didn't help matters either. He was always hanging around, offering to help and quivering with what I took (correctly, I believe) to be barely suppressed sexual passion. Happily, Diana took no notice of him but, even so, I was often quite anxious, wondering what he might get up to when I was out working and Diana was alone in the flat.

The only advantages the place had were that it was comparatively close to Fleet Street and there was a good, cheap Italian restaurant just down the road where we ate most of our evening meals when we were home together.

Before we moved to Victoria we had spent Christmas at my parents' house in Edgware. Mum and Dad weren't there; they, along with Valerie, had gone to Los Angeles and from there to Australia, where my father directed *The Summer of the Seventeenth Doll*, based on a play by Ray Lawler and starring Ernest Borgnine, Angela Lansbury and John Mills.

Christmas Day, then, was celebrated by just Diana, Rick and me, and pretty disastrous it was. We'd decided we wouldn't have a turkey this time but went for a goose instead. We bought it from the butcher's shop beneath our Hendon flat; it was horrible. It seemed to have been fed on nothing but leftover bits of fish, so the taste and smell of fish permeated its entire body. When you bite into goose, you expect . . . well, I'm not sure what; I'd never eaten it before, nor have I since, but you don't expect your mouth to be filled with the taste of cod that had clearly died of old age.

Anyway, we went from Hendon to Edgware to Victoria and, fairly swiftly, though hardly swiftly enough, from there to Datchworth.

What brought about this move – our final one – was sheer chance. My father's agent, Leslie Linder, had been looking for a house in the country and had heard about three sets of farm labourers' cottages in Datchworth, which were set for demolition. There was nothing wrong with them structurally (well, as it turned out, there was with one lot, ironically the one Leslie Linder had earmarked for himself, which had to be torn down), but they had no electricity or indoor sanitation, just water and gas laid on. The lavatories were outside, at the end of the garden. There were four tiny cottages in each block and, until recently, despite the primitive circumstances, they had all been occupied. Now, the owner had decided to demolish them unless somebody was prepared to convert each lot into what was described as 'a habitable dwelling', in which case they were available on a 999-year lease at £30 a year.

Leslie, having chosen his own ill-fated block,

suggested that Dad, who was looking for a country cottage where he could go to write and read scripts, might be interested in one of the others. But as Datchworth is only about 20 miles from Edgware, Dad couldn't really see the point; a country cottage that is practically next door to your main home is hardly fulfilling its purpose. So he suggested that, since it was about time Diana and I had a home of our own, we should take it on.

At first we weren't that keen. Okay, Datchworth is not much more than 30 miles from the centre of London and thus within easy commuter distance either by car or train. But we'd been brought up in towns and cities; why would we want to isolate ourselves in the sticks? Dad said, 'Well, at least come and look at it,' and so we did, though at first glance we weren't impressed. As we drove up the lane on a dank, gloomy afternoon towards the block of cottages he had in mind for us I saw a huge rat running along the gutter. Oh great, I thought, the whole place is overrun with vermin.

The cottages themselves, though set in quite a large, pear-shaped piece of land divided roughly into four then-neglected gardens, looked unprepossessing. The rooms – two up, two down plus a kitchen – were tiny. In one of the cottages, we were told, a family of twelve had lived, presumably sleeping in shifts, and that particular one plus its neighbour were to become our sitting room. We took them on partly because of their proximity to London but mostly because we felt it was time we got a foot on the property ladder. Today, most 25-year-old couples, unless they're remarkably fortunate, can only dream of such a thing, but then it was taken for granted that this was what you did.

We hired a gifted architect, Martin Priestman, who lived just down the road, to design the conversion for us. The local council helped us out with a £400 grant on condition that we lived there for three years, and, altogether, the conversion cost us £2,600. What we ended up with was a long, narrow, four-bedroom house with a large sitting room, a small kitchen, a dining room and a study, and about a quarter of an acre of garden.

When I look at the price of four-bedroom houses now, I still find that astonishing. I know it was more than fifty years ago, but has there ever been any other fifty-year period in history when money became quite so drastically devalued? Even as recently as the turn of the millennium a millionaire was regarded as enviably wealthy; now he's just thought to be quite comfortably off.

I had £600 saved up and used most of that, along with the council grant, as an advance payment for the builders, but Diana and I were so naive about such matters that we had actually moved into the house before I even considered getting a mortgage for the rest. Eventually, an agent for the Co-op insurance company came to call and asked how much I earned. What Diana earned wasn't taken into account; good Lord, I was the master of the house, wasn't I? She was a mere chattel.

'£28,' I said.

'What – £28 a month?'

'No, £28 a week.' And here's another example of how the value of money has changed: he was much impressed. 'Oh, well,' he said, '£28 a week, no problem.' If you multiplied that by ten now, you probably wouldn't get a mortgage on a garden shed.

Datchworth was a revelation to us. We moved in on the anniversary of D-Day, 6 June 1959, and both took time off to decorate the place because, even on my princely salary, we couldn't afford to hire professionals. Diana did the wallpapering and turned out to be rather good at it, while I did the painting, at which I was actually rubbish, though if you didn't look very closely the result wasn't too bad.

The other job I had – one Diana flatly refused to contemplate – was emptying the Elsans, the temporary lavatories in the sheds at the end of the garden. Not only had the builders failed to remove them, they had also used them copiously and left them filled to the brim. In that blisteringly hot summer, my task was to dig a series of holes in the baked earth and then, oh so carefully, empty those stinking cans into them. While I was doing this I was observed with some interest by our neighbour's pigs, which, in the absence of a fence worth mentioning, had wandered into the garden.

Around this time I was harbouring strong doubts about the wisdom of moving to the country. For much the same money we could have bought a neat little house in the suburbs where neither pigs nor Elsans featured.

But then we encountered the kindness of strangers. Jane Priestman, Martin's wife – who went on to become design manager for the British Airports Authority and director of architecture and design for the British Railways Board – was the first to pop in as we sweltered through the decorating. When you're fed up with doing that, she said, come to our house and have a glass of wine on the lawn. Since at that time we had neither wine nor a lawn – all we had was earth – we were deeply thankful. Then others, people we'd never met, came up with offers of food and drink. Some of them, admittedly, were simply curious; they'd watched the conversion through all its stages and, because half the house was taken up by the sitting room, they thought this must be a studio and we must be artists, though they were decent enough not to hold that against us. But in their offers of help they were certainly genuine, and this was a kindness we had never encountered in our moves around London.

The house-warming was a bit of a disaster. We'd decorated the, as it were, public rooms and fitted them out with brand-new Wilton carpet, to which we'd added some very decent second-hand furniture bought, under my mother's shrewd guidance, at an auction house in Baker Street. The place looked pretty good, we thought, and we invited a few locals and our Fleet Street friends to help us celebrate our new home. The Fleet Street mob turned up en masse, bearing vast amounts of booze, which was fine except that on this, of all days that summer, it had poured with rain, and by the time we got rid of the last of the guests, way into the early hours of the next morning, you could hardly see our new carpet for mud.

Aeron had come up from Torquay to help with the moving in and one morning she woke us at about seven o'clock, announcing that there was a giant at the door. So there was – Roger Higgs, who was about six foot six and ran the farm down the end of the road. We'd first encountered him in one of the village pubs – downtown Datchworth consisting, as any self-respecting English village should, of two pubs and two shops, one of which doubled as a post office – where, unlike other people who take the weight off their feet by leaning on the bar, he was given to leaning on the ceiling. That's the kind of thing you notice.

On this particular day he had delayed his visit till 7 a.m., on the grounds presumably that, as far as he, a farmer, was concerned, it was already mid-morning and a decent time to make social calls, in order to invite us to dinner. So began a lifelong friendship with him and his wife, Jean, though the initial dinner was a little baffling for townsfolk like Diana and me. We ate splendidly – Jean was a terrific cook – then retired to the sitting room for coffee and conversation, whereupon Roger fell asleep. Jean, serving the coffee, gave him a shake. 'Roger! Are you going to pour liqueurs?' Roger opened one eye. 'No. You do it,' he said, and went back to sleep.

'God, are we that boring?' Diana wondered as we walked home. But I don't think we were. It was just that we weren't accustomed to clocking on for work much before 11 a.m. whereas for a dairy farmer, who was up before dawn to milk the cows, 10 p.m. was probably way past his bedtime.

We invited them back for a return match, which started pretty well. We had drinks and nibbles and chatted away until about nine o'clock, when Roger's head was already beginning to nod a bit, and Diana said: 'Jean, do you think it's time to put the chicken in the oven?'

Cooking was an art she still hadn't mastered.

Even more than the Priestmans, it was Roger and Jean who dragged us into village life. Through them we became involved with the local church, largely because throughout her life Diana was a devoted – though like most people often doubting – Christian, and Roger introduced me to the cricket club. I hadn't played much since I left school and was therefore rather surprised when my interest in joining the club was greeted with much enthusiasm. God, they must be hard up for players, I thought, until I realized that what they were actually hard up for was transport. I was one of the few people in the village who had a car and could therefore be relied upon to take at least three other players to away matches. For some time I was never too confident about getting a game at home but I was damn sure I'd be picked for the away fixtures.

Roger and Jean swiftly became our closest friends in the village and one year the four of us spent a brief holiday in the Pas de Calais. In the course of this we went one day to St Omer. It was market day, and some kind of pop music was being played on loudspeakers all over the town. Now, Diana loved music, especially the classics but not excluding good pop – the Beatles (she was an early fan) and almost anything by Cole Porter or Jerome Kern. But – and here was the point – she liked listening to music when she chose to listen to it, not necessarily when someone else chose to play it. She couldn't abide music/muzak in restaurants, pubs or lifts. A pianist tinkling away in the background was acceptable; anything blaring out of a machine was not, and on this day she found the constant thrum of pop in St Omer particularly irksome.

So, without explanation, she marched us all to the tourist office, where she approached the girl behind the reception desk and said: 'Kindly turn off the music.'

I was horrified; so was Roger, and he was not a man who lacked chutzpah – he had been known to request a discount at a filling station if he paid for his petrol in cash.

The girl, clearly, couldn't believe what was being demanded of her, so Diana repeated the request, rather more firmly this time.

'But, madame,' said the girl to this young, determined but obviously demented Englishwoman, 'I cannot do that.'

'Perhaps not,' said Diana, 'but you must know someone who can. Call him and tell him to turn it off at once. It's very irritating.'

Sadly for her, however, this was one occasion when she simply couldn't win and, after a bit of a Mexican stand-off, she led us back into the music-filled air of St Omer and, once we'd retrieved our car, to the road out of town.

One way or another, then, we were sucked into Datchworth life. It had never been our intention to stay there. Our plan had been to stick around until we were no longer obliged to repay the council grant, sell at a profit, move to somewhere a bit bigger and do the same kind of thing all over again. Financially, that would probably have been the smart way to go. All being well, we could have ended up in a small manor house somewhere, lording it over the local peasantry.

But fairly soon we decided that Datchworth was the place for us. We liked the village, the people, the countryside, the friendliness, the total lack of bullshit – except perhaps in the literal sense – that country life has to offer.

So we stayed and, some eighteen months before she died, Diana and I threw a party to celebrate our fiftieth year in the same house. In the meantime, we had certainly made alterations – we had built another front room and a scullery, extended the kitchen, bought some more land as a protection against possible building development in the fields behind us and added a new hallway, plus a downstairs bedroom and its en-suite bathroom.

Staying put was the wisest move we could have made. Shortly before she died Diana wrote to a friend, telling him that, from her perspective, the first two years of our marriage were pretty awful, adding that one of the reasons she stayed with me at that time was that being on her own again and having to face the penury that came from renting a flat and buying the Plainmoor house for her mother was more than she could contemplate. Even in those days I'd never seen myself as some kind of milch cow, but I suppose paying a rent and buying a house were easier on two salaries than one.

'But,' she also added, 'when we moved to Datchworth things got better, so much better that the last fifty years of marriage have been ones I thank God for.'

Both our daughters were born in the house, Samantha in 1962 and Emma in 1964. Diana refused to have her babies in hospital, blithely ignoring the tooth-sucking disapproval of her doctors and nurses as they pointed out the dangers of giving birth at home. I think one of her reasons was that, according to the ancient hedger and ditcher who lived next door at that time, there was a curse on the former cottage in which our main bedroom was situated, the curse being that only daughters, never sons, would be born there. That suited Diana fine, because daughters were what she wanted; she firmly rejected even the possibility that she might have a boy. And, as usual, she had her way.

As time went by she sold the house in Plainmoor and bought Aeron a bungalow about a hundred yards down the road from us. Furthermore, to relieve ourselves of worry about where we might go when our 999-year lease ran out, we bought the freehold on our property. Then my parents moved from Edgware to a sixteenth-century cottage on the outskirts of Stevenage, the nearest town to Datchworth, before moving on to our neighbouring village, Knebworth. Meanwhile, my brother, Rick, and his wife, Christine, had come briefly to Datchworth before themselves shifting to Knebworth, and my sister, Valerie, and her then husband, Bernie Williams – who produced, among other films, *Barry Lyndon* for Stanley Kubrick, *Dirty Rotten Scoundrels* and *Charlotte's Web* – bought a house in Welwyn, the next village but one.

One Christmas Day, while he was working on *Barry Lyndon*, Bernie had a phone call from an excited Kubrick. 'Bernie, get over here. I've had a great idea for the movie.'

Bernie said: 'Well, yeah Stanley, but, you know—'

'Who are you talking to?' asked Val.

Bernie put his hand over the mouthpiece. 'It's Stanley. He wants me to go and see him now.'

'Give me the phone,' said Val, and snatched it from him. 'Mr Kubrick,' she said into it, 'it's Christmas Day. Fuck off,' and slammed the receiver down.

To do him justice, Kubrick – who, I imagine, hadn't been told to fuck off by anybody for a very long time, if, indeed, ever – immediately called back to apologize.

At one point, I thought about buying a much bigger property in the heart of the village, but Diana wouldn't have it. 'I love this house,' she said. 'I don't want to move anywhere.'

When the girls grew into teenagers and started bringing boyfriends home we had the room that is now my study built on to the front of the house. It'll be a place for the girls to entertain their friends, Diana said, and that was fine by me, because I was fed up with picking my way through the sitting room, trying to avoid long male adolescent legs with big boots sprawling out from my favourite armchair.

As to the boyfriends, Diana had this sage advice: 'Whatever the girls bring home, try to love it,' she said. 'You never know, it might end up as our son-in-law.' As it turned out, what the girls brought home might not always have been easy to love but, generally speaking, was certainly likeable, though there was one exception – a very good-looking and in all other respects charming young Mormon, who not only objected to Samantha wearing make-up but objected to Diana wearing it, too, which really cheesed her off.

Soon after we moved to Datchworth, Diana left the *Herald* and joined a magazine, the *Woman's Mirror*. She was at last the mistress of her own house, we both knew now that we wanted to stay together and have a family, and it was time, she felt, to lay down a solid basis for our marriage. Bad enough for one of us to be flitting around and in and out of the country; if we both continued to do it we were pretty sure we'd end up, like so many of our journalist friends, in the divorce courts.

Maybe if we were deciding such a thing now I'd be the one to stay home and freelance, because it was a great sacrifice for her. She was the better and more respected journalist (I was still a gossip writer) and she loved the *Herald* and her workmates there. But this was before Women's Lib had taken a hold, and any notion of equality of the sexes was still in its infancy, in journalism as elsewhere. Generally speaking, in the early sixties, any woman who rose to be editor of the fashion pages on a daily newspaper was already bumping her head against the glass ceiling. Besides, a man who, in those days, gave up the day job to run a house would have been regarded, at best, as a wimp.

So I stayed put and she settled into the less demanding life of a magazine writer and, in the long run, that was probably the best course of action for both of us. At the *Herald*, Diana had been given very little opportunity to write feature articles and develop her writing style; her bosses saw her only as an excellent news reporter. But now she was writing features all the time, first for the *Woman's Mirror* and then, when she went freelance, for magazines like *She*, and, eventually, two of the articles she turned out produced ideas for books.

I, meanwhile, was finally able to break free from the shackles of the gossip column to become first the *Mail*'s showbusiness reporter, then its showbusiness editor, a job that might sound a bit grand but wasn't. All it seemed to mean was that I got a little more money and in return was held responsible for any showbusiness story that other papers got and we didn't. Certainly I had no influence; I was never invited to the daily news conferences, and no other executive ever sought my opinion.

Very much on the plus side, though, was the fact that, as showbusiness reporter, I shared an office with two of the most influential men in my life, and indeed Diana's

– Bernard Levin, the finest newspaper columnist of his day, first on the *Mail* and then *The Times*, and Julian Holland, a feature writer who later became editor of the *Today* programme on BBC Radio 4.

For some time they pretty well ignored me, but one day I found myself interrupting one of their regular intellectual arguments to make a point that contradicted both of them. At first they could hardly believe my effrontery. They turned and glowered at me. 'Pray explain yourself,' said Bernard, icily. So I did and there was a brief silence, then, 'You may have a point,' he said. After that they included me in their conversations and I learned so much from them both. I'd thought I was reasonably well educated; at school I'd read many of the English classics, as well as quite a few of the works of the French and German masters in the original language. I mean, hey, I could have gone to Cambridge. But now I realized I knew little or nothing about literature or the theatre, not to mention politics, and these two guys were exceedingly well versed in all these things. They shared their knowledge with me, listened to what I had to say, discussed it and argued with it; for me it was like having tutorials and I would go home and pass on what I had learned to Diana.

Thanks to Bernard and Julian, we, hitherto an apolitical couple, became supporters of the Labour Party and remained so for a good few years, though I must say I did feel a little betrayed when, years later, on

The Times, Bernard revealed himself to be an enthusiastic convert to Thatcherism. But, what the hell, nobody's perfect, not even Bernard.

As a sad postscript to my friendship with Bernard, sometime in 1995 he invited me to lunch. A very posh restaurant in Chelsea, because Bernard was a gourmet; he loved good food and fine wines, though he ate and drank sparingly. Some months earlier I had taken him to lunch at the Ivy, and there he told me he had not been well. He refused to say what was wrong but said he had been undergoing tests in hospitals. He looked and sounded fine, so I didn't take too much notice.

But that day in Chelsea he told me he was suffering from Alzheimer's disease. I asked how it manifested itself, and he said: 'Well, as I walked across the room to where you're sitting I realized I couldn't remember your name.' He and I had been friends for thirty years. Then he added: 'And yesterday when I was booking this table I had to write down what I wanted to say, otherwise as soon as I got on the phone I would have forgotten.'

It was the most touching and in many ways the most awful lunch I ever had with Bernard. On every previous occasion, no matter who had been present, he had dominated the conversation and everyone else had listened happily, because he was not only the cleverest man I have ever known personally but also a brilliant and witty conversationalist. But this time I had to take the lead. Whenever we exhausted a particular subject he fell silent and waited for me to introduce another, and if I was slow to do so an awkward silence would ensue. It was very hard to take in, because this was a fiercely intelligent man who not only had a photographic memory but, as I had often told him, was never short of a few thousand words. Now he had hardly anything to say.

When the meal was over I saw him into a taxi – Bernard's automatic reaction whenever he stepped out of doors was to yell, 'Taxi!', because he never took public transport – and it was only after he had gone that I realized, belatedly, that this lunch had been his way of saying goodbye, and that, indeed, was how it turned out.

For a while we kept in contact by mail but, after a time, his letters dried up and I didn't see him again until 2003, when I was asked to write a foreword to a reissue of his first book, *The Pendulum Years*. By then I knew from mutual friends that the Alzheimer's had taken full effect. His publishers had arranged a small launch party at the Reform Club in Pall Mall, and Bernard was there. He looked much the same as ever, whiter of hair but otherwise trim and smart, and, with a glass of red wine in his hand, he was studying the paintings on the wall. The publisher took me over to him. 'Bernard, this is your old friend Barry, who wrote the foreword.' Bernard shook my hand, smiled and said, 'Well, well, well,' and it was quite obvious that he hadn't the faintest idea who I was.

A little later I saw him for the last time at David Frost's annual summer party. He was sitting alone at a table in the garden with a plate of canapés and his usual glass of red wine. Samantha was with me. She and Emma had known Bernard since they were little girls. He had given them the complete works of Dr Seuss and an enormous paint box with which he had urged them to create murals on our sitting-room wall, much to Diana's and my alarm. Once, I had found both girls in his office at the *Daily Mail*, where he was trying to teach them to type.

Now Samantha said: 'Come on, let's go and talk to Bernard.' He greeted us with a warm smile but, once again, it was clear that he didn't remember either of us. Samantha tried hard to jog his memory by reminding him of incidents from the past, but the only response was another smile and a 'Well, well, well.' We were both close to tears when we left him.

Bernard died in August 2004, twelve days short of his seventy-sixth birthday. He was one of the nicest people I have ever known, a wonderful friend and one of the biggest influences in my life. In those last ten years before he died he had been extremely lucky to have as his partner the journalist Liz Anderson, who took the greatest care of him. But, God, when you see the effect Alzheimer's has on someone with as brilliant a mind as his, you can't help railing at the cruelty of it.

* * *

On Christmas Eve 1962 Diana and I went to Midnight Mass at the church a couple of hundred yards down the road, she heavily pregnant, dressed in a red top and black trousers and looking like an enormous robin redbreast. Early in the morning of 28 December, during an almighty blizzard, Samantha was born.

I'd wanted to be present for the birth, an unusual desire in those days long before the idea of New Man or Metro Man had been conceived. But the midwife, who had struggled through the snow to be with us, would have none of it. Aeron was there to help and that, the midwife thought, was quite enough; childbirth, in her opinion, was very much not a man's business and, though I disagreed, arguing that both literally and metaphorically I'd had at least some input, as soon as Diana went into the last throes of labour I was banished from the bedroom with orders to boil as much water as I possibly could. When I returned, announcing triumphantly that there was now enough hot water to fill every bath in the neighbourhood, I discovered that a) none of it was needed and b) Samantha was already among those present.

While all that was going on, a friend called round to invite me out for a drink. I told him what was happening upstairs. 'Oh, Christ,' he said, and went off to the pub by himself.

Later that day Tony and Roger celebrated Samantha's birth by building a snowman for her in the garden.

Such was the severity of that winter that it was still there, somewhat diminished but still recognizably a snowman, at Easter.

However, when Emma came along on 29 February 1964 I was ready for the midwife (the same one) and her dastardly tricks to keep me out of the way. I resolutely refused to boil any water. Instead, I stayed by Diana's side as she clutched my hand fiercely enough to draw blood and roundly cursed me and every male who had ever lived for causing the agony she was going through. My reward was to be there for Emma's birth, for the miracle of seeing someone enter the room who hadn't come in through the door. I wasn't sobbing but there were tears streaming down my cheeks and, more than ever, I regretted not having been there when Mamf was born. (Incidentally, Samantha has always been known in the family as Mamfie because when we showed her off proudly, newborn, to a friend and her two-year-old daughter, Mamfie was as close as the child could come to pronouncing her name.)

Diana had been a fierce proponent of Women's Lib even before the idea was given a name. She didn't go along with all that bra-burning stuff, thinking it silly, but she firmly believed that women should at least have equality, or preferably superiority. When the idea became a movement she went on a Women's Lib march in central London alongside a friend who was carrying a loaded handgun with which, she said, she would 'shoot the balls off any policeman who gets in our way'. Diana rather approved of that – she could be very militant when she liked – but, fortunately, the police simply oversaw the march from a respectful distance and didn't interfere.

Luckily for the peace of our home, I agreed with Diana – not about the handgun but about the unfairness with which women were treated and the lack of opportunity that was offered to them – although there was one time when I began to have doubts . . .

In 1966 Barclays Bank introduced the first credit card, the Barclaycard, in the UK, and I was sent one. I hadn't asked for it; it just came. It had a year's duration and my credit limit was £100. With pride I showed it to Diana.

'Where's mine?' she asked.

'You haven't got one.'

'But we have a joint account. I should have a card!'

'I know,' I said. 'But I'm the man. What can you do?'

Immediately, she sprang into action, bombarding Barclays with irate letters demanding a Barclaycard at once. At first the poor fools took a lofty attitude, explaining that they weren't issuing cards to women who had joint accounts, but they had no idea who they were dealing with. Each reply made Diana angrier than before and led to another fierce letter until, eventually, they caved in, as I had always known they would. When you're up against a force of nature, the only sensible option is to run for cover, and Barclays did – at the end of the year they sent her a Barclaycard with a bigger credit limit than they had given me.

'Ha,' she said, triumphantly, when it arrived. 'See? I've won.'

'Yes,' I said, 'but where's mine?'

'Oh, you haven't got one,' she said. 'They only sent one to me.'

This, I suppose, was Barclays' way of getting their own back on her – by making me suffer. I had to go to them on bended knee and beg to be given a card of my own. They agreed but, from that day on, my credit limit was always lower than Diana's, although for a long time I earned the bulk of the money that went into the account. They would raise her credit limit unasked, but they never did that for me. Once, I received a sharp note telling me that 'Your Barclaycard is in an arrears situation.' They were dunning me for £10. They never dunned Diana. They wouldn't have dared.

Datchworth has changed a fair bit since 1959. There are no longer pigs wandering into our garden. The turkey farm down the road where, in the early years, Diana and I used to go on Christmas Eve to select our bird for the holidays and watch while the women plucked and prepared it, has gone, to be replaced by a small estate of pleasant houses, an allotment and an area of common land where people walk their dogs and the kids play football. The Tilbury has become an excellent gastropub, coexisting amicably with the Plough across the road, where the villagers tend to gather, especially on nice summer evenings, to drink and chat; the post office is now a tearoom; the village shop, which over the years has had a pretty up-and-down existence, is run splendidly by Pinkie and Pardi Kumar; the sports club has acquired a powerful rugby section, which seems to have more pitches than the Harlequins, and infilling, so far carefully done, has meant the population has risen by a few hundred. But, essentially, it's still the same place, the friendly village where Diana and I decided to put down our roots and raise our family.

None of this could have been predicted on the anniversary of D-Day, 1959, when we moved in, but then neither could our professional fortunes, which were to develop in ways neither of us could possibly have imagined.

7

Paperback Writers

WE BOTH BEGAN our fiction-writing careers on the same day some time in 1958. We were spending the weekend at Aeron's house in Devon; the weather was dull, Aeron was at work in the chemist shop and Tony and Roger were out doing whatever kids did in an age before Facebook and computer games claimed their entire attention. So we settled down in the sitting room, each armed with a thick notebook, to begin our first novels. Diana's last remark as she moved closer to the fire, opened her notebook and got out her pen was: 'Move over, Tolstoy.'

A couple of hours later, having filled a good many pages, I glanced up to see her sleeping peacefully in her armchair. I tiptoed across and looked over her shoulder at her notebook. It was open at the first page, at the top of which was written 'Chapter One'. Just that, nothing else.

'Good start,' I said, when she woke up. Nothing wrong with it, of course; it was just a bit incomplete, as novels go.

'Well,' she said, 'you can't rush these things.' Nor did she; it was to be another five years before she published a book, and that was a work of non-fiction, *The Stately Ghosts of England*.

I, however, plugged on and within a few months had filled three fat notebooks and completed my first novel, a police procedural. All I had to do now was type it out, add, subtract and rewrite here and there, and bingo! Bestsellerdom, here I come. Unfortunately, at this stage I lost the middle notebook. I think it fell out of my car one day. Whatever. The middle third of my novel was gone and, unlike T. E. Lawrence, who left the only copy of his original version of *The Seven Pillars of Wisdom* in a taxi and then wrote the whole damn thing all over again, I didn't have the heart to go back and re-create the missing stuff. Just as well perhaps; it probably wasn't any good, anyway.

But the result was that, when it came to publishing, Diana beat me to the punch. *The Stately Ghosts of England* came out in 1963; my first book, a thriller called *The Matter of Mandrake*, didn't appear until four years later.

Stately Ghosts was inspired by an article Diana had written for a magazine, a piece she didn't really want to write. The editor had asked her to accompany a clairvoyant, Tom Corbett, to Longleat, the stately home of the Marquess of Bath, where Tom proposed to sniff out any ghosts that might be lurking around. Diana wasn't at all keen; she didn't believe in ghosts and, come to that, she didn't believe in clairvoyants either. But it was a job – another day, another dollar – we had two small daughters to support, to say nothing of a dog, two cats, a couple of guinea pigs and a pair of mortgages, and so she went.

Tom was the first pleasant surprise – a big, bluff, hugely likeable Irishman built like a rugby forward who was openly gay at a time when, because of the law, you normally had to unlock a closet to find a gay person. He made no extravagant claims for himself; he was not a spiritualist or a medium, he merely said he had been born with some extra psychic sense that enabled him to feel, hear and see vague sights and sounds that weren't apparent to most of us. He hadn't asked for it, he said, he just seemed to have it, and there were times when he thought he might have been happier without it.

Diana was sceptical even of that, until they got to Longleat, where the marquess's son Lord Christopher Thynne took them to an allegedly haunted corridor. Tom walked slowly along it, sniffing the air, then shook his head. 'No, sorry,' he said. 'Can't find anything.' Then he walked on to another corridor, where he stopped. 'Ah,' he said. 'This is your corridor. Something dreadful happened here.'

Only then was it revealed that Lord Christopher had originally taken him to the wrong place, presumably to test him out, and that the one Tom had identified was indeed the corridor in which people felt chilled, uneasy or even alarmed. This, it seemed, was the corridor in which an earlier marquess had allegedly walled up his errant wife or mistress and left her to die.

Diana was impressed; even more so when Tom sniffed out another room where people claimed to have felt a kind of other-worldly presence. I'm not sure how much she actually believed in ghosts thereafter, but she certainly kept an open mind about them. More than that, really – I think that, if forced to choose between belief, scepticism and disbelief, she would have come down on the side of belief.

I was impressed with Tom, too. After his Longleat success he had told Diana that he was planning to investigate occult phenomena in other stately homes and wondered whether she would care to join him, a Boswell to his Johnson, with a possible book in mind.

By now she was intrigued enough to agree, and on one of their trips I went with them. Diana was driving, Tom was in the back seat. After a while he leaned forward and, though knowing little about me except that I was a by no means celebrated journalist, said: 'I've been studying your head, Barry, and I think you'll do very well.' A pause, then . . . 'But not necessarily through writing.'

The latter was a bit of a downer; I didn't want to do well at anything except writing. But, in a sense, it could be argued that he was right. I've written a number of books (this is my twenty-first) and though, for the most part, they've been gratifyingly well received by critics and those who use public libraries, they haven't gone down that well with people who actually buy books. Put it this way: if I'd had to rely on them to make my living, I'd have a very unhappy bank manager.

Such a modicum of success as I have enjoyed has come through television. This is not to say that I regard myself as successful, because everything I've ever done I feel I should have done better, if only I'd known how. Success, I think, is probably more evident to the beholder than to the person who is, apparently, enjoying it.

But was Tom entirely right? That I survived for thirty years on TV, reviewing films, presenting an Olympic Games chat show in 1988 and writing and presenting numerous documentaries I cannot entirely attribute to my stunning good looks and sex appeal (when I was younger, of course), though, naturally, they were present. Good Lord, yes. Did I not, after all, for a time share with Melvyn Bragg the label of 'the thinking girl's crumpet'? (I prefer to forget the fact that, when they learned of this, Diana and both daughters rolled around in uncontrollable mirth.)

No, I choose to believe that it was what I said rather

than my mere presence on television that brought me some kind of following among the viewers. And what I said was what I wrote. Every word of every script I ever delivered on TV or radio was written by me. Indeed, at the BBC and later Sky, I laid down a stern rule: anyone could change my script so long as it was me. I've been known to throw tantrums if a single word was altered without my authorization. Not that this proves anything, of course. There have been television performers who were barely able to write their own names and could only read scripts provided for them by a producer or researcher, but a kind of celebrity still attached to them, such is the power of the medium itself. Even so, I like to feel that despite what Tom said my writing did contribute to whatever it was I achieved.

Anyway, Diana and Tom visited eleven of England's stately homes, discovering a variety of hauntings and ghosts, stately or otherwise, and their researches led not only to the book but also to a television movie. One day, an American TV producer, Frank De Felitta (who later went on to become a novelist himself), knocked, unannounced, on our door and, when Diana got home, she found him there chatting to her mother. He'd read *Stately Ghosts* and liked it, he told her, and wanted to film it. What did she think?

What she thought, as she later said, was that she couldn't understand why on earth he wanted to do it. As far as she was concerned, the book was simply a piece of accomplished journalism, no more. But what the hell ... 'Okay,' she said, and, ever the thoughtful hostess, asked him what he'd like to drink. A dry martini, he said. Diana, who, after her Fleet Street days, hardly drank at all, had probably never even seen a dry martini but, by chance – and it was by chance, for in those days our drinks cabinet was pretty bare – we had the ingredients, give or take the olive or cocktail onion. She poured a hefty slug of gin into a tumbler and said, in her innocence: 'Same amount of vermouth?'

De Felitta was horrified. This was in the sixties, when Americans hadn't really discovered wine and tended to accompany even the finest meals with beer, scotch or dry martinis. 'No, no!' he yelled. He seized the vermouth bottle from her and did little more than wave the cork over the gin.

Once they'd got that settled, the relationship proceeded smoothly. De Felitta wanted Tom in the film but not Diana; he wanted Margaret Rutherford instead. That suited Diana perfectly; she hated even having her photograph taken, let alone appearing in front of a TV camera. Nevertheless, she was somewhat dubious: why would anyone as prominent as Margaret Rutherford want to appear in this kind of TV show? De Felitta said he'd arrange all that and, somehow, he did. Perhaps his budget was a lot bigger than Diana realized. The only proviso was that, along with Rutherford, he would have to provide a role for her husband, Stringer Davis. They

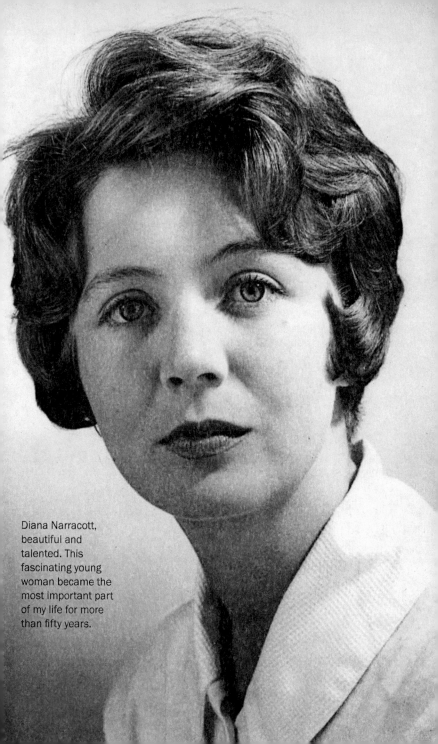

Diana Narracott,
beautiful and
talented. This
fascinating young
woman became the
most important part
of my life for more
than fifty years.

Above: Our wedding day in 1957. That's Richard Attenborough, giving Diana a kiss, and he in turn is being kissed by Donald Sinden. Next to Donald is Sheila Sim and Donald's wife, Dinah, is standing next to me.

Below: Diana and me, soon after we were married. It's no surprise that many a man fell in love with her, but, happily, she chose to stick with me.

Dee with her younger brothers, Tony and Roger, to whom she was devoted.

Left and below: Our beautiful girls, Samantha (known to all as Mamfie) and Emma. Dee always wanted daughters and, as usual, got her way!

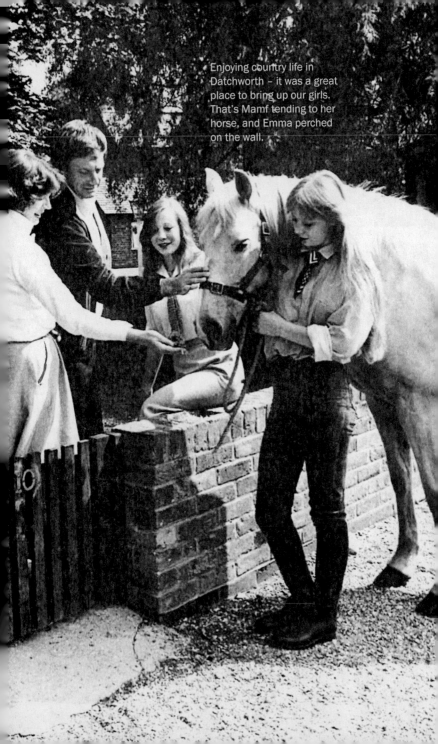

Enjoying country life in Datchworth – it was a great place to bring up our girls. That's Mamf tending to her horse, and Emma perched on the wall.

The Norman clan

Above (from left to right): My sister Valerie, my brother Rick's wife Christine and Diana, clutching the champagne.

Below: Me (now clutching the bubbly) with, from left to right, my father Leslie, Valerie, my mum Betty and my brother Rick.

From the mid-seventies onwards, we holidayed in the Catalan village of Sant Martí d'Empúries. We loved it there, and were one of a group of families who would return every year, even long after our children had kids of their own.

Above: Dee with Emma and her son Bertie.

Below: Mamf relaxing with a coffee.

Right: Charlie's first day at school.

Below: In our kitchen in Datchworth with Bertie.

Bottom: Harry takes on Grandma at Scrabble. Woe betide anyone who beat Diana at a game – she really didn't like to lose.

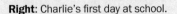

had been married since 1945 and, though Davis admitted to an unrequited infatuation with John Gielgud, he and Rutherford were devoted to each other, to such an extent that she insisted he must have a part – usually very small – in whatever film she made, mostly appearing in the credits as 'Mr Stringer'. From his point of view, this was just as well. His career consisted almost exclusively of roles his wife procured for him. Anyone running a book on the world's worst actor would surely have Mr Stringer among the favourites. If he had only one line to speak, there was a very fair chance he would forget it, or at least have to repeat it several times before he got it approximately right.

So the film was made. Rutherford, with Stringer stringing along, turned up to the locations swathed in scarves and sweaters – or, as Tom put it: 'Nothing left at home in the woolly line, dear.' Diana went to most places with the film unit, writing the occasional bit of script and breastfeeding Emma as she did so. She even gave Stringer one line, but 'the sweet man kept mucking it up so eventually we had to leave him out'.

The end product was really rather good, a nice mixture of humour and serious examination of the supernatural. If it had been seen in Britain at a time when there were only three TV channels, at least two of them attracting enormous audiences, who knows what might have happened? Almost certainly, it would have increased the sales of the book and sharply enhanced

Diana's profile as a writer. But, alas, it was shown only in America. Despite Rutherford's presence, no British TV company was interested in taking it. So the book came and went pretty well unnoticed and with far more modest sales than it deserved.

Increasingly, I believe that literary success is a matter of chance and often has little to do with the author's ability as a writer. Timing – bringing out the right story at the right time – is vital; witness the phenomenal sales of *The Da Vinci Code*, one of the most clumsily written novels I've ever read. And having the right friends, established writers who will extol the virtues of your work, whether it's good or not, can be a big help, too.

Diana never enjoyed either of those things. She wrote only the books she wanted to write, not being interested in trying to second-guess what kind of specific topics prospective readers might be looking for. And she never courted the friendship of more successful writers who might have been in a position to give her a shove up the ladder. It's true that a number of well-known authors, among them bestsellers such as Tess Gerritsen and Kate Mosse, wrote in high praise of her books, but she never asked them to do that and in most cases had never even met them. So the eventual success of her various historical novels, particularly in America, Canada and Germany (where there seems to be a surprisingly keen interest in British history), came from glowing reviews by strangers and, most importantly, word of mouth among her readers.

As for ghosts, well, on that subject I have two quite meaningless anecdotes to recount. But let me set the scene for the first one: in 1968–9 the England cricket team was to tour South Africa, where apartheid still reigned. The touring team was named but, to general shock and indignation, Basil D'Oliviera was omitted. Dolly, who was what was known as a 'Cape coloured' South African, had come to this country to play cricket for Worcestershire and qualify for England. He had done that so well that in the Oval Ashes Test of 1968 he had scored a century. Even so, he wasn't selected to tour his native land. The reason for his omission has never been particularly clear, but it probably had much to do with the then hidebound Marylebone Cricket Club, which controlled the English game, believing, along with most right-wing politicians, in the fatuous idea that the only way to do anything about apartheid was to keep 'building bridges' with South Africa's bigoted and intransigent Nationalist government. So Dolly was overlooked in order not to upset anyone. Then Tom Cartwright, one of those chosen to tour, dropped out because of injury, and even the MCC could now find no reason to ask anyone except Dolly to take his place. Dr Balthazar Vorster, South Africa's prime minister, was outraged. *Hey, man, you expect us to welcome a bloody kaffir, treat him like a white man, let him travel on the same planes, trains and coaches and stay in the same hotels as white men, man? No, man, this is a deliberate political insult, man.* Impasse – only resolved when the whole tour was cancelled, a great decision in that it led to South Africa being ostracized by the entire sporting world (except for occasional bunches of unthinking idiots who went on a few 'outlaw' tours) until 1991, when apartheid was abolished.

However – 1968 and the Dolly Affair. The *Daily Mail* sent me to Worcester in a chauffeur-driven car to ask him how he felt about it. On the way there, we passed a large cemetery. I have no idea where it was or why I took any notice of it, but I did. On the way back, as we approached the cemetery again, I distinctly saw a little old woman, shoulders bent and dressed all in black, walk out of the gate and start to cross the road to the field on the other side. I was so alarmed that I was about to say to the driver: 'For God's sake, stop or you'll run her over.' But before I could speak we'd gone past her without slackening speed and without hitting anything, and when I looked back there was no sign of her. The driver had obviously seen nothing. But I had; I know I had.

What, if anything, that signified, God knows, and my other anecdote is just as inconsequential. One evening at home, I said: 'Do you know, I could swear I just saw someone pass the back door.' Diana and the girls barely looked up from whatever it was they were doing. 'Oh,' they said, more or less in unison, 'that was probably the ghost.'

'What ghost?' I said.

'Haven't you seen him before?' Diana asked. 'He often passes by.'

I was unconvinced. Clearly, it was some kind of shadow, a trick of the light. But a few years ago, as the whole family – Diana, me, the girls, the grandsons – were sitting down to Christmas lunch, I glanced up and saw as clearly as I saw those at the table a little old man with a head of curly white hair passing by the kitchen window. What the hell? I thought. Who'd come visiting at this time on Christmas Day? So I leapt up, opened the door, looked out – and there was nobody there.

The family watched all this with curiosity. 'What are you doing?' they asked, so I told them.

'Ah, that's just the ghost again,' one of them said, and asked someone to pass the potatoes.

There was one other odd experience Diana and I shared. One year, we visited Fontevraud Abbey, near Chinon, where she was doing some research. We toured the abbey and then went outside to look down on it, alongside a group of French tourists with their guide. Suddenly, we heard the sound of plainsong, so startling and unexpected that we looked around to see where it was coming from. It was certainly not from the abbey – there was no choir of monks in there – and not, as far as we could see, from anywhere else. The sound was clear and beautiful but seemingly only Dee and I heard it; none of the French tourists even looked up and the guide carried on with his patter.

Make what you will of all that. I can't find any meaning to it. But, on both occasions, I know what I saw, and, like Diana, I now neither believe nor disbelieve in ghosts, but I'm keeping an open mind.

Towards the end of her life Diana was cheerfully given to telling interviewers that she had spent the sixties writing fiction 'with a child on each hip'. A nice image, but not at all accurate. Her second book, *Road from Singapore*, again a work of non-fiction, did not come out until 1970, by which time Samantha, pushing eight, and Emma, six, would have been a bit cumbersome to carry on each hip.

Early in the decade, in fact, when she was pregnant with Mamfie, Diana took a job as unit publicist on a film called *The Man Who Finally Died*, a thriller starring Stanley Baker and Peter Cushing. What makes this mildly curious is that though for much of my professional life I've been closely associated with films, of my most immediate family – parents, brother, sister, wife and children – I'm the only one who never actually worked in the movie industry. (Well, Emma and me, really, because Mamf once had a small role in a low-budget British film.) Diana said her most memorable contribution to the publicity was to write a press handout in which she referred to a man being 'shot in the Urals', thus causing every male member of the crew to wince and clutch themselves and say they couldn't think of a more painful place to be shot.

But, for the most part, what she was doing during the sixties and into the next decade was historical research. She had become fascinated by Henry II and his introduction to England of the jury system. She loved Henry and hated the supposedly saintly Thomas à Becket, who, she felt, simply had it coming when those knights did him in. Indeed, I believe it was Henry, not me, who was the real love of her life, though I like to think I came a fairly close second. So she spent at least a decade reading everything she could find about him, to such an extent that I'm convinced she ended up knowing more about twelfth-century England than anyone else, Oxbridge professors included. But that was the way she was: if a subject interested her she had to learn everything there was to know about it. And perhaps that was the difference between us as writers: she had to become an expert, while I took the more journalistic approach of learning just enough about a subject.

Eventually, all the knowledge she acquired was to prove invaluable in her career as a novelist and, if asked, she would probably have said that was the whole point. But I'm not so sure. Memory tells me that, for several years, she was doing the research purely for its own sake, because it fascinated her and because it took her mind off the occasionally tedious business of running a house and caring for two small children. In my re-collection, I asked her one day: 'What are you going to do with all this stuff you've learned about the twelfth century? Write a book or something?', with Diana reply-ing: 'Dunno. I might,' and not sounding too sure about it. She'd probably deny that any such conversation ever took place, and maybe she'd be right, although she was always good at erasing inconvenient facts from her memory.

My own first book *The Matter of Mandrake* was published in 1967. This was a time when Ian Fleming's James Bond and Len Deighton's nameless and far more working-class hero of *The Ipcress File* were all the rage, and I'd decided to write a thriller whose protagonist was, well, neither the one nor the other but sort of in-between. For some time I got no farther than this basic notion; I had no sort of story in mind, just a vague idea, but then a strange thing happened: one morning I woke up with the entire plot – beginning, middle and end – fully formed in my mind. Amazing what the sub-conscious will do for you. I got up and immediately started writing, drove to the station, got on the train and wrote some more. Same on the way home from work – scribbling away in a notebook. Back home, I had a quick meal, and, mindful of the disaster of the earlier lost notebook, typed out everything I'd written. This went on for six weeks; whenever I had time to spare, I wrote. And then it was finished and I sent it off to an agent, the urbane and courteous George Greenfield, who was everything I'd expected an agent to be in an era when publishing was a more laid-back and gentlemanly business than it has perforce become. God knows where I'd got his name from, not that it matters: the important thing was that, bless him, he liked the book.

Unfortunately, several publishers didn't and it was several months and a fair bit of rewriting on my part before it was accepted by W. H. Allen. The critical response both here and in America, where it was also published, was good; the public one, alas, disappointingly less so. Still, I did get a very nice review in *The New York Times*, where the writer pointed out that the plot revolved around the making of an epic movie called *The Life and Loves of Pontius Pilate* and wondered how come Hollywood hadn't actually made such a film already. When you consider that, around that time, they were turning out movies like *King of Kings*, in which Jeffrey Hunter played Christ with shaven armpits, I feel he had a point. (As it happened, I went to Spain to report on the making of that film and found that Hunter had to be treated with something close to reverence. He wasn't giving interviews and walked about the set apparently studying the Bible with deep concentration, and we hacks were forbidden even to approach him, which led one journalist to sneak up on him saying, 'Excuse me, Mr Hunter, I know I'm not allowed to talk to you but may I kiss the hem of your garment?')

I followed *The Matter of Mandrake* with *The Hounds of Sparta*, another thriller featuring the same protagonist, Paul Baker, a journalist-cum-part-time espionage agent, and that went pretty well, too. But then I made a big mistake. W. H. Allen wanted me to continue with the Paul Baker series in the hope that it might gradually acquire a respectable readership, but instead I wrote a comedy, *A Series of Defeats*, and they emphatically didn't want that. In fact, nobody wanted it for several years, though I thought it was pretty good. So did George Greenfield but because we couldn't find any takers we parted company, and it wasn't until another agent, the excellent Michael Shaw of Curtis Brown, took me on that my writing career was kick-started again.

A Series of Defeats got its title from George Orwell's wise remark that any man's life when seen from the inside is simply a series of defeats. Megalomaniacs might disagree, but I do believe that to be true. It's not a matter of regrets about what one did or didn't do, or might have done if only. Professionally, I have none of those; for me, it's more a question of looking back at what I've actually done and wishing, as I've said before, that I'd done it better. Except in my early days in journalism, especially on the *Daily Sketch*, I've, happily, had few complaints about my work – well, give or take bitter moans from people whose films I didn't like. Immodest though it probably is, I can even say that I've been complimented quite often, but though the compliments pleased me I usually felt I didn't really deserve them: everything I wrote or said always seemed to be better when it was in my head than when I put it down on paper or spoke it aloud. And maybe that's not a bad thing, because what it meant was that I always tried to do it better next time. It wasn't a question of striving for perfection; that's impossible, anyway. It was more a realization that you can't rest on your laurels; you can't say, 'Hey, that was good. I've cracked it now,' because, as soon as you do that, you're on your way down and out.

8

Of Mice and Men

THE SEVENTIES BROUGHT about dramatic changes in our lives. For a start, the *Daily Mail* kicked me out or, to put it more accurately, in March 1971 it merged with its sister paper the *Daily Sketch*, turned itself into a tabloid and made half the joint editorial staffs of both papers redundant, my friend Julian Holland and myself among them. I blame Julian for this; he had fallen out with Arthur Brittenden, editor of the *Mail*, and so when Arthur and David English (editor of the new *Daily Mail* and soon to be Sir David) sat down to decide who should be retained and who should not Julian was first on the 'got to go' list, and I, because I was his close mate, swiftly followed.

My initial response to redundancy (a comparatively rare event in any industry back then) was that I thought it deeply insulting. I'd been.with the paper more than a dozen years, had become one of its better-known writers and was its showbusiness editor. What had I done to deserve such ignominy? What I had done, as I discovered later, was to hang around long enough for my salary to rise for the first time to £5,000 a year, and the new paper didn't want costly people like that on the staff. What it wanted was young, keen men and women, who may or may not have been as good as 37-year-old veterans like me but were certainly cheaper.

As it turned out, of course, making us redundant was quite the nicest thing the *Daily Mail* ever did for Julian and me. Make no mistake, we had both very much enjoyed our years with the paper but, in a marvellous way, life became even better after it booted us out. Julian returned to the BBC, whence he had come to try his hand in journalism at the London *Evening News* and then the *Mail*, and swiftly rose to the editorship of Radio 4's *World at One* and later the *Today* programme.

To give it its due, the *Mail* was pretty good to us redundees. It gave us a year's salary plus a month's pay for every year we'd worked there, plus whatever we'd contributed to the pension scheme, so I walked away with something over £7,000, not bad money in those days and enough, with care, to keep the family going for maybe eighteen months. In addition, we were allowed to hang around the office for the rest of the month, use the paper's facilities to try to find other jobs and were not called upon to do any work unless absolutely necessary.

Even so, redundancy hurt. It threw me into a mood of dark despair and a feeling of total lethargy. I didn't want to look for a job; I didn't want to do anything. Only on one occasion could I even bring myself to seek an interview with an executive of another newspaper, and that came to nothing because, through no fault of his own, the editor in question kept me waiting for half an hour and I walked out in a black sulk without even seeing him. Despite all those big bylines and my picture in the paper, nobody offered me a job, though I would have eagerly taken almost anything that came along. It was as if, as far as Fleet Street was concerned, I had ceased to exist. Even in the *Mail* office the atmosphere was odd; those who had been retained were suddenly not too eager to be seen in the company of the people made redundant, as if redundancy were a communicable disease.

At home things were no better. I simply moped around, too depressed and frankly scared even to contemplate my future and how I might go about shaping it. Diana, though, was wonderful. Never did she reproach me for my idleness or urge me to get off my backside and just do something. Instead she made what she believed to be a very helpful suggestion. She called the girls to her and said: 'Look, your father has lost his job. There's not going to be much money coming into the house so we've got to make economies. You'll have to use less lavatory paper in future.'

Well, at eight and seven, they were most hygienic little girls and did tend to go through toilet rolls at a remarkable speed, but, even so, there were other economies I might have suggested first. On the other hand, I suppose we had to start somewhere.

And as for there not being much money coming into the house, Diana was dead right. The only work I had when finally the *Mail* cut the umbilical cord was an agreement to write one television review a week for *The Times* at a fee of £15. No way could we live on that.

With not even a sniff of a staff job coming my way, I was perforce obliged to freelance, something I'd been idly contemplating for a year or two in the realization that I'd got about as far as I was likely to go at the *Mail*. Progress for me there could only have come through climbing the executive ladder, of which I had been on the bottom rung, the problem being that in my case all the rungs above me had been cut off. Nobody at the paper, including me, saw me as higher executive material. In fact, I didn't even want to be an executive. I didn't regard myself as a leader of men but, at the same time, I didn't want to be a follower of men either; I just wanted to do my own thing, which was to write. Freelancing would afford me that opportunity, but I had always put off treading that route, partly because I didn't have sufficient capital to keep me going while I tried to establish myself and partly because I lacked the courage and self-confidence. I wasn't at all sure I could hack it.

Now, however, I had to try, and thanks to the redundancy pay-off, I did at least have enough money to pay the mortgage and put food on the table for a reasonable amount of time, whether I earned anything or not.

So, finally, I roused myself from my lethargy and started putting myself about, offering ideas to newspapers and magazines, some of which were accepted and some of which were not, and taking any commission that was offered, no matter how pitiful the pay. And, gradually, it began to work. For the sort of pittance I would have sneered at a few weeks earlier, I wrote numerous pieces for the Central Office of Information. Also, my very good friend Wally Fawkes, superb jazz clarinettist and equally superb cartoonist under the name of Trog, asked me to take over from George Melly as the writer of Wally's strip cartoon *Flook* in the *Daily Mail*. George had been writing it as social satire for twenty-five years but had now decided to go back on tour as a jazz singer. Wally and I, being far more reclusive than George and knowing little of the London social scene, turned it into a political satire and, this being the era of Richard Milhous Nixon and, later, Watergate, I introduced characters such as Millstone Dixon, marshal of Dodgy City.

But what turned out to be my most significant break

of all came thanks to the blessed Bernard Levin, who phoned me one day to suggest that I contact Alastair Hetherington, editor of the *Guardian*, because: 'I never told you this but when you were made redundant I wrote to him and said that if he was thinking of recruiting anybody from the *Mail* you were probably the best bet because you were least likely to be drunk all the time, throw up on his carpet or try to rape the managing director's wife.'

Glowing with the warmth of this encomium, I went to see Hetherington, whom I had never met before and who quite clearly knew nothing about me except what Bernard had told him. It was a weird interview, which took place around ten o'clock one night in his office. Alastair, it turned out, wasn't looking for a showbusiness writer like me but a holiday-relief leader writer, which was bizarre in itself. I cannot think of any other serious newspaper in the world that would contemplate dragging a complete stranger in off the streets to write its opinions for it. But that's what Alastair was after and, eventually, when we had both acknowledged that I was quite unfit to write about grown-up stuff like politics, foreign policy or the economy, he took me on to provide the fourth leader, the humorous one. I did that three times a week for about four months, until all the real leader writers were back from their holidays and Alastair couldn't afford to keep an extra one, even a freelance, on the payroll. Happily, however, thanks to the features editor, Peter Preston (later himself to become editor of the paper), I was able to segue my leader writing into a weekly humorous or even satirical column, which I continued to write for pretty well the rest of the decade.

Now the offers came flooding in: John Higgins, arts editor of *The Times*, asked me to write film and theatre interviews as well as my weekly TV review; *Cosmopolitan* wanted think pieces; so did *Punch*, edited by Alan Coren, the best and funniest humorous writer of my time. Suddenly, unexpectedly, I was working up to seven days a week, enjoying it more than I had ever enjoyed my work before and even earning more money than I had ever earned before. Not that it was easy; the *Guardian* column taught me that writing humour is one of the hardest things in the world. I vividly remember one particular day when I sat down at my typewriter (this was before anyone had computers) at about nine o'clock in the morning to do my stuff and was still there at six in the evening, knee-deep in discarded pieces of paper and a blank sheet in the typewriter. Throughout the day inspiration had eluded me. At this point Diana came into the room and said gently: 'Stop, relax. Come and have a glass of sherry and start again tomorrow.'

This I did and, the next day, from somewhere, an idea came to me and I wrote my column. Which was duly received, as everything I wrote was received at the

Guardian, by someone who said, 'Yeah, okay, that's fine.' It was all I ever got from the *Guardian* – no laugh, not even a smile, just 'Yeah, okay, that's fine.' But they kept taking the stuff and so I kept writing it. And in this Diana was invaluable. She was my sounding post. Whenever I finished my column I would ask her to read it; if she was amused I would hand it in to the paper; if she wasn't I'd tear it up and start again. In a way, I suppose, I wrote my columns for her.

Sometimes she was my muse as well. One day, I was writing my *Guardian* piece when she crept into my study and, working her way through the loads of washing she had put in there to dry, whispered: 'Sorry, I won't interrupt. I just want to put this down for the mouse.'

Well, it was true that we had been invaded by a mouse, a refugee from the fields outside, and were rather keen to get rid of it. But what she was putting down for it was a mousetrap loaded with a slice of salami.

'Do you,' I said, 'have reason to believe that this is an Italian mouse?'

'No,' she replied, 'but we're out of Cheddar and I'm not giving it any of my Brie.' I abandoned the piece I'd been composing and wrote about her and the mouse instead.

Another column was inspired by her sudden decision to establish a compost heap at the end of the garden.

She was disgusted, she said, by the amount of food we simply put in the dustbin; now it would go on the compost heap and thereby enrich our garden. She became quite obsessive about this. One day, I was finishing my lunch when she said: 'You're not going to eat all that, are you?'

'Well,' I said, 'I thought I might.'

'No, you've had enough,' she said, and she took my plate away and emptied it on to the compost heap. After a while I reckoned the compost heap was eating better than the family; she threw everything on to it, including, inadvertently, a carving knife. So, one day, when she piled all the leftovers on to a dish and instructed me to take it to the compost heap, I said: 'No way. I'm not going near that thing – it's got a knife.' All grist to the *Guardian* mill.

But what I learned from this was how subjective humour is. Sometimes – not often – an idea would spring fully formed into my mind and I would work on it, revise it and polish it until I knew it was hilarious and would hand it in ('Yeah, okay, that's fine'), confident that it would receive an enthusiastic response from the readers. And nothing happened, nothing at all. Other times I would knock out a piece out of sheer, last-minute desperation ('Yeah, okay, that's fine') and the readers – those who bothered to write in, anyway – were hugely complimentary.

I couldn't understand it. I would compare the piece I

thought was particularly funny with the piece the readers liked and try to work out the difference. I never did. What I learned from that was never to laugh at my own jokes, however hilarious I thought they might be. Much later, when I was on television, studio directors would say: 'What you just said, that was very funny. Why didn't you smile when you said it?' And I would reply: 'Because it's not up to me to decide what's funny. It's up to the viewer.' What it boils down to is this: if something, written or spoken, makes you laugh, it's funny; if it doesn't, it isn't – no matter what its creator might have thought – and there's an end to it.

The *Guardian* was a terrific newspaper in those days; it had a sense of fun, which no paper (including itself) has ever shown since. Its misprints, of course, were legendary – that's why *Private Eye* refers to it as 'the Grauniad' – and it loved wordplay and puns. Derek Malcolm's adverse review of the Charlton Heston movie *Antony and Cleopatra* appeared under the headline 'The Biggest Asp Disaster in the World', allegedly causing the deeply wounded Chuck to skulk in his London hotel room for two days; and the report of a football match involving Crystal Palace, in which a player called Queen was involved in some kind of fracas, evoked the even better headline 'Queen in Brawl at Palace'.

We humorous columnists, among us Richard

Boston, would each fill a long single column at the top of which was a blotchy photograph of the author. One day, Richard decided he was fed up with his own photograph and wrote a whole piece complaining bitterly about it. The following week, his column, devoted to an entirely different subject, was headed by a photo of Telly Savalas; the week after that, again on a different subject, it appeared under a picture of Brigitte Bardot. No explanation was ever offered for this and, as far as I know, nobody ever asked for one. If you read the *Guardian*, it was assumed by staff and reader alike that you were a member of an exclusive club and merely took whatever it did, however apparently eccentric, in your stride.

9

Radio Days

MY COMPARATIVELY well-heeled redundancy had led me to one important decision; at the *Mail* I had been pigeonholed as a showbusiness writer, but now I was free to explore myself and my limitations, to find out just what I could and couldn't do. For that reason, I continued to take every offer that came my way. For a while I wrote and broadcast a 'Letter from London' on the BBC World Service, and discovered that I wasn't bad on the radio. My great friend Ron Atkin, who had left the *Mail* before me and become sports editor of the *Observer*, asked me to report on a First Division football match, so I did, and that was okay, too. Then he asked me to do sports interviews, and I went off to talk to the likes of Geoffrey Boycott, the world speedway champion Ivan Mauger and the boxers Tommy Farr and Henry Cooper. I asked Henry about his philosophy regarding his opponents and he considered the matter thoughtfully before replying: 'Well, put it this way – you don't want to 'urt yer man, I mean you don't want to *maim* 'im – you just want to 'it 'im on 'is chin before 'e 'its you on yours.' So there you have it – the Noble Art in a nutshell.

And since we've got on to the subject of boxing, in 1988 when I was presenting a nightly chat show about the Seoul Olympics on Channel 4, I asked one of our guests, the Scotsman Jim Watt, former lightweight champion of the world, whether he was ever scared of any of his opponents. 'Scared o' my opponents?' he said. 'Ah was scared o' men wi' tattoos!'

Another of the guests was the former world heavyweight champion Frank Bruno, a great big, likeable teddy bear of a man. Well, he was until I asked him about his forthcoming world title bout with the fearsome Mike Tyson. Frank was very upbeat about it, confident that he would win. 'But what if you don't?' I asked him. 'What if you lose?' Suddenly, his happy smile was replaced by a most menacing scowl. 'You're putting negative thoughts in my head,' he said. 'I don't like people putting negative thoughts in my head.' I took one look at his immense bulk across the table and decided that no more negative thoughts would emanate from me. Okay, I chickened out; you'd have had to be Mike Tyson not to.

By January 1972 I was pretty well established as a

reliable, versatile freelance journalist – columnist, critic, interviewer and writer of a popular and respected strip cartoon. I'd even tried my hand at radio reasonably well. Television, though, was another matter. I'd been on three times – the first time back in the sixties when Anglia TV had invited me to be a judge on an amateur talent programme it was running. This started pretty well but then, for some reason, my mind drifted off, until suddenly I became convinced that someone had just asked my opinion, so I gave it. Unfortunately, I was wrong; at this moment of all moments, nobody wanted my opinion or indeed that of any of the other judges because the presenter had just started her carefully honed piece to camera and I butted in, on an entirely different subject, even as she was getting into her stride. This did not go down at all well; in fact, I'm not sure that she or the producer of the show talked to me again for the rest of the evening, although we all went out to supper afterwards. In any event, I was never invited back.

My second TV appearance was on a Granada programme presented by Michael Scott in Manchester. It was a show on which a trio of TV critics (the experts) discussed television over the previous week in front of a studio audience, who had been hand-picked by Gallup and was actively encouraged to join in the debate. On this occasion I had been asked to take part in a discussion of the way television covered sport.

Dutifully, I spent a week watching every sports programme I could find and turned up in Manchester
pretty well prepared, I thought, until the producer said:
'What did you think of the film last night?'

'What film?'

'The one on BBC2, of course, about British troops
going into Northern Ireland.'

'Oh, I didn't see that,' I said. 'I was watching
Sportsnight on BBC1.'

'Oh, Christ,' he said, horrified. 'Didn't anyone tell
you? We're not doing sport this week, after all; we're
discussing last night's film on BBC2.'

'Well, not to worry,' I said. 'Get me a tape of it and I
can watch it now. Plenty of time.'

Ah, but here was the snag: they didn't have a tape and
it was too late to get one. What to do? 'Read the reviews
in the papers,' he said, 'and busk it.'

Which is what I did, and it was a disaster. The
Gallup-selected audience knew at once that I was wing-
ing it and every time I opened my mouth I was shouted
down by someone in the studio who knew far more
about the BBC2 film than I did. There were apologies
all round afterwards, and by way of recompense I was
invited back a couple of months later, but this time, for
some reason, there were not just three critics but a
whole bunch of us and I failed abjectly to distinguish
myself.

So that was it, I thought. Television is emphatically

not for me; that is one thing I certainly cannot do. But then, early in 1972, I was invited to be among about a dozen critics asked to go on the BBC2 show *Late Night Line-up* to discuss television over the previous year. Naturally, I was not at all sanguine about this but, since I knew all the other critics pretty well, I reckoned it might not be that bad and neither was it. None of us was an experienced telly performer but because we did know each other we were all pretty relaxed – certainly, I was more relaxed than I had been on my previous three appearances – and it turned into a rather enjoyable verbal punch-up in which we all interrupted and argued with each other.

I felt better about television after that but I still had no desire to be on it, except perhaps as an occasional pundit. I had great respect for those people on TV who, in my opinion, did it well, but being one of them was nowhere on my wish list. So I was mildly astonished when, a couple of days later, I had a phone call from a man I had never heard of called Iain Johnstone, who introduced himself as the producer of *Film '72*, a film review programme then shown only in London and the South-east and used as a vehicle to find new faces for TV. This meant that it changed its presenter every few weeks, and what Iain wanted to know was whether I'd like to be one of those presenters. He'd seen me on *Late Night Line-up*, he said, and didn't think my appearance would frighten the audience too much, liked my stuff in the *Guardian* and wondered whether I could take the same kind of irreverent approach to film criticism as I did to writing about politics and current affairs.

I was decidedly dubious about that but he persuaded me to have lunch with him at Television Centre, then gave me a camera test, which I appeared to pass, followed by another test to see whether I could read autocue (a very simple task, as it turned out), announced enthusiastically that I was 'a natural' and gave me the list of films he wanted me to review the following week.

The contract, when it arrived, didn't seem to endorse anyone's opinion that I was a natural; it was for three weeks with an option, exercisable only by the BBC, for another three weeks. This didn't exactly fill me with confidence but, curiously, I didn't care. I'd already decided that television wasn't for me except as an occasional nice little earner in a guest capacity. So I decided to use my three weeks on *Film '72* merely as a way to familiarize myself with the way TV worked so that I would be better equipped the next time anyone wanted to employ me as a sort of rent-a-pundit.

This 'sod it, I'm a writer, not a telly person' approach served me well, I think. Although the morning after my first appearance on *Film '72* our next-door neighbours told me (with perhaps just a touch of *Schadenfreude*) that they could see how tense I had been, they were actually quite wrong. I wasn't tense at all and everything went rather smoothly, so smoothly in fact that Iain immediately took up the three-week option and later extended it, so that my first engagement on the programme spread to nine weeks, after which various people – including Joan (now Baroness) Bakewell – all tried their hand at it. Over the next twelve months I returned a couple of times for six-week stints although, during one of them, my connection with the show nearly came to an untimely end.

During a weekly review board at which the BBC executives discussed what had been on the box in the last seven days, Paul (now Sir Paul) Fox, controller of BBC1, flew into a rage and declared that I had been wearing a wig on TV the previous night; he wasn't having wigs on his channel and I was to be got rid of. Fortunately, Iain, who was present, was able to assure him that I wasn't wearing a wig, that I never wore a wig and was simply having a bad-hair day. Paul has since denied that any such conversation took place, but Iain told me about it the day after it happened, so with all due respect I prefer to believe what I was told then rather than what Paul remembered forty years later. Anyway, whatever was or was not said on that occasion, early in 1973 Paul declared himself fed up with all the revolving presenters on the film programme and suggested they offer the job to me full-time.

By then I was ready. At that time, far more than now, as the Internet seems to be taking over every other medium, television was clearly the place to be. I enjoyed seeing the films and writing the scripts and, sometimes, when I thought it had gone well, even being on the box. It didn't bring me much fame back then – the programme was still only seen in London and the South-east – but I genuinely wasn't interested in fame; I don't think many of us were in those days, especially those of us who were also journalists. We knew we weren't there because we were startlingly good-looking but because we were reckoned to be reasonably expert in one area or another and we simply enjoyed showing off our expertise and our opinions and getting paid for it. If so doing brought with it a modicum of fame, well, that was an agreeable but by no means vital by-product. It seems to be different nowadays; everyone wants to be a celebrity and therefore wants to be on television, because if you turn up on the box a couple of times the tabloid press automatically dubs you a celebrity. You don't actually have to do anything, still less know anything worthwhile, you just have to look good on the box and glory in being famous for being famous.

Even as a full-time presenter, I regarded television as only a part-time job. Opt-out programmes like mine, programmes, that is to say, that were shown in a limited number of areas, could vanish as quickly as they had started. Indeed, one summer when the film programme was off the air its slot was taken over by *Going Places*, which I co-presented with Sarah Dickinson. It was a magazine programme which covered leisure and holiday activities and its producer was Pat Ingram, who by then had also taken over the film show from Iain Johnstone. *Going Places* was not a bad programme, actually, and one that included various quirky items. One day I was invited to hit a martial arts expert as hard as I could in the stomach because, he said, he could control his muscles in such a way that I couldn't possibly hurt him. I wish I could say I laid him flat with a vicious blow to the solar plexus but in fact the best I could manage was a weak right jab. I wanted to hit him much harder but I simply couldn't. If he had hit me first I would probably have walloped him, but when someone actually invites you to hit him it's impossible to summon up the enthusiasm. Well, it was for me.

There was another occasion when we went to Calais and Sarah and I sat on a hot, sunlit restaurant terrace chatting to each other, for the benefit of the camera, across a table that bore a huge dish of mouthwateringly delicious shellfish – lobsters, crabs, oysters, prawns, shrimps, whelks – you name it. I was desperate to fall upon this stuff, but by the time the producer, cameraman and soundman were happy – 'Could you go back over that bit?' . . . 'Sorry, sorry, we'll have to go again. A car backfired' . . . 'Hang on, could you just mention . . . ?' – it was reckoned that all this glorious food had been in the sun too long and was no longer safe to eat. We probably ended up with a hamburger somewhere.

However, nice little programme that it was, *Going Places* only lasted one summer and, as I saw it, if that could be dropped, so could the film programme. Therefore I kept on with my newspaper work, although after I'd been on TV regularly for a while I gave up writing television reviews for *The Times*, since there was obviously a conflict of interest. I also gave up *Flook* after three years and was succeeded by Barry Took. But I kept on with the *Guardian* column and other commitments until pretty well the end of the decade.

Apart from anything else, I needed the money, at first, anyway. I forget what *Film '73* paid me for my first three-month contract, but it was certainly less than three figures per show. The programme took up three days and three evenings a week: on Day One, I would see three or four films at private cinemas in the Soho area; on Day Two, I would go into Television Centre to write the script, then see another film; on Day Three, I would rehearse and record the programme and see a fifth (or sixth) movie. If I'd given up the freelance journalism to concentrate on this it would have left a big hole in my income.

Mind you, the BBC fees did get better. One day I went into the Curtis Brown offices to discuss a projected novel with Mike Shaw. When we'd finished that he asked who was looking after my television interests. I said nobody was, that I was negotiating the fees myself. I really didn't enjoy doing that. Then, as now, the BBC was much given to pleading poverty, producers arguing pitifully that they had to make their programmes on minimal budgets and that even a fiver or so here and there could mean the difference between breaking even and going into the red. I did kind of wonder where all the licence fee money went even then, although of course it's much clearer now. These days we have a pretty good idea of the lavish salaries paid to a few presenters, managers, director-generals, controllers of channels and the heads of this, that and Stacked Chairs, and it's obvious that with such a hefty annual outlay plus the fat pensions these people are going to receive there can hardly be much left to make programmes.

But that day Mike said: 'Why don't you go and talk to our Sue Freathy? She looks after people's TV and radio interests.' So I did. Sue turned out to be an attractive, laid-back and very likeable young woman who asked how much I was being paid for the film programme and when my contract was up for renegotiation. The latter, in fact, was about to happen soon. Sue took a note of the money I was paid and the renegotiation date and said: 'Why don't you leave it with me? Let me see what I can do for you.'

I was happy to agree, reasoning that even if she only got me the same money and took a 10 per cent commission on that, the commission would come out of income tax so I'd hardly be any worse off. Plus I'd be spared the embarrassment of squabbling about money with the people I worked with, producers close to tears as they tried to make ends meet.

About a week later Sue phoned me. 'This is what I've arranged with them,' she said, and named a fee roughly twice what I'd been getting so far. As I was to learn later, television accounts departments loved Sue personally but hated dealing with her professionally because she was the toughest negotiator they knew. What she had done showed how badly you can be screwed if you try to make deals yourself. My advice to anyone trying to break into any medium of communication is: get a good agent.

The film show crept on to the national BBC network in 1976 – fortnightly, alternating on Sunday evenings with Melvyn Bragg's book programme *Read All About It*. The TV critics took no notice, which suited me very well, because I was still learning my trade. Presenting a television programme adequately is comparatively easy, especially if you've written the script yourself and can read autocue without swivelling your eyes from side to side, which itself is pretty simple: the autocue moves at the speed of the reader and there are never more than about a dozen words on the screen at any one time. Doing it well, however, is another matter, and I realized that quite early on. It involves a lot of thought and self-criticism. I never enjoyed watching myself on the box because, though I'm sure I'm not without vanity, I never possessed that degree of narcissism, but I made myself do it to discover what I was doing wrong. Did I look serious enough or too serious? Was I fidgeting in my chair or waving my hands about too much? What had swiftly become clear to me was that unless I was a little nervous, unless the adrenaline was flowing before the recording began it wouldn't be any good. Only once did I go into the studio feeling so totally relaxed that afterwards I thought: Hey, that's got to be the best show I've ever done. It turned out to be one of the worst; I was so laid-back that it looked as if I couldn't be bothered.

Before *Film '76* achieved network status there'd been another big development in my career: I had come – and gone – as co-presenter of the *Today* programme on BBC Radio 4. This was another opportunity, which, like the film show, had been offered to me in a most casual way. It was 1974. Robert Robinson, who had been John Timpson's co-presenter for several years, had decided to retire and *Today* was looking for someone to take his place. Several people were tried out, Melvyn Bragg, Malcolm Billings, Desmond Lynam and myself among them. My offer came via a phone call from Alistair Osborne, then deputy editor and later editor of the programme.

Would I care to have a go at it? . . . Well, yeah, but I haven't done much radio . . . Never mind. Come into Broadcasting House tomorrow evening, see how we prepare for the next day's show, stay overnight, then come back into the studio early next morning and watch John and Malcolm do their stuff.

That's what I did. I stayed across the road at the Langham, now a very posh hotel but then owned by the BBC to house, among other things, the BBC club and to provide bedrooms for the use of staff who had to be in early.

I was in at 5 a.m. and dutifully watched proceedings – the briefing of the presenters by the various producers, the writing of the scripts, the actual broadcast itself – whereafter Alistair said: 'There you are. Quite simple, isn't it? Come in early on Saturday morning and present the show by yourself.'

It's hard to believe now. This was Radio 4's flagship news and current affairs programme and there was I, a film critic and humorous/satirical columnist with little experience of radio and none whatsoever as a political journalist, being commissioned to present it. Admittedly, at that time, the Saturday programme was deliberately more trivial than the rest of the week's offerings (later, not least at my insistence, it became much more serious) but, even so, important political news could as easily break on a Friday night or Saturday morning as at any other time in the week, and I was expected to handle it.

Surely nowadays people are given much more training than I was offered? If not, they ought to be. Still, my debut seemed to go okay and soon I was turning up not only on Saturdays but two or three times during the week to co-present, usually with John, sometimes with Malcolm, once or twice with Melvyn but somehow never with Des. At the same time, I was continuing with the film programme, the *Guardian* column, for a while with *Flook* (before I handed over to Barry Took), and other bits and pieces of journalism. Oh, yes, mine was a busy week, so busy that I even gave up playing cricket for Datchworth in order to have some time with Diana and the girls.

This went on for nineteen months until Brian Redhead, the former editor of the *Manchester Evening News*, was signed as John Timpson's regular co-presenter and Mike Chaney took over from Alistair as the editor of *Today*. With Brian and John turning up Monday through Friday I was now only needed for the Saturday show, and not for long on that. As the new editor, Mike presumably felt he had to show he was the new broom and do a bit of sweeping clean. Of the presenters, the only one he could sweep out was me, because I was the only one on a short-term contract, so I was duly swept out. Many years later when interviewed for a book about *Today* he said he had done this because I was too busy to come in on Friday evenings and do interviews for the next day's show. This was total nonsense – before me, no Saturday-morning presenter had ever come in on Friday evenings; I was the one who insisted on doing so.

Mike, a very amiable bloke, handled the firing nicely and we parted on pretty good terms. I didn't see him again for some years until we met at a reception in Broadcasting House and he took me to one side and said: 'You know, I think I fired the wrong presenter.'

Anyway, that was the end of my connection with *Today*, except as an occasional interviewee, although in the eighties Julian Holland, by then the editor of the programme, invited me to come back as an occasional presenter. I was very tempted but also very busy and, with reluctance, I turned him down.

My association with radio resumed again in 1977 when John Lloyd, the inventive creator of TV shows like *QI*, devised *The News Quiz* and asked me to become the first chairman, charged with overseeing and trying to keep in check the likes of Alan Coren, Richard Ingrams, Clive James and Clement Freud as they made funny – and often very rude – comments on the week's news and its makers. But for me that job only lasted a couple of series, because in the same year Brian Cowgill, then controller of BBC1, asked my producer, Barry Brown, and me to make five documentaries in America under the generic title *The Hollywood Greats*. So when I was asked to do the next series of *The News Quiz* I said I'd be delighted to do the first three shows, but after that I'd be away.

This information was passed on to whoever was controller of Radio 4 at that time and he apparently flew into a rage, demanding to know who the hell I thought I was to dictate my terms to him. No way was he going to have me coming and going whenever I felt like it. Find someone else, he said. In fact, I wasn't dictating anything to anyone – I was simply telling it like it was; I was already contracted to make the documentaries and there was no way round it. Nevertheless, the offer to do three programmes was apologetically withdrawn and I was replaced – just as I had been as the writer of *Flook* – by Barry Took.

Even so, they couldn't keep me off the radio. In 1977, the same year I was ejected from *The News Quiz*, I was in California filming the first series of *Hollywood Greats* when I had a call from Roger Macdonald, a producer with whom I had worked often on the *Today* programme. He wanted to know whether I knew anything about transport. When I said 'nothing except that I use it a lot', he promptly signed me up to write and present *Going Places*, not a revival of the earlier television show, but a current affairs radio programme he had devised to take a close and critical look at all forms of transport in Britain. What he wanted, he said, was someone who could bring a completely unbiased mind to the subject. I said I could do better than that, I could bring total ignorance, and he said that was best of all.

And so the seventies ended. Quite a decade for me. In addition to everything else, I had also had five books published. *Tales of the Redundance Kid* was a collection of newspaper and magazine pieces, mostly from the *Guardian*. 'How nice,' said a journalist friend, somewhat sniffily, 'to earn money all over again from one's juvenilia.' Oh, journalists can be very jealous people, as I swiftly learned from the snide reviews my film programme occasionally received from Fleet Street people I thought were friends but who felt that if, for heaven's sake, I could make it on television then so could they, and they could do it better, and it wasn't fair that I'd been given the opportunity and they hadn't.

That book, along with one by my good friend and cricket historian David Frith, was given a launch party at the Oval on the first day of the England–Australia Test Match in 1975, and I have a clear recollection of Dennis Lillee and Jeff Thomson standing side by side in the pavilion like a pair of swing doors. If you've only seen them on the pitch you have no idea of the breadth of shoulder and chest of really hostile fast bowlers.

Redundance Kid was followed by three novels – *End Product*, *A Series of Defeats* and *To Nick a Good Body*, all published by Quartet, a company newly formed by four disaffected executives from Granada publishing, chief among them William Miller.

William was splendidly eccentric. I used to meet him in his office above a shop in Goodge Street, where we would chat about this and that until he said: 'Let's go and play table football.' This was the heads-up that serious business was now about to be discussed. In the nearby pub where we played table football several drinks would be consumed. William was a dab hand at the game and I was pretty useless, not that it mattered: if the positions had been reversed I would still have made sure he won because, let's face it, if you're trying to sell a book to a publisher, you're not going to thrash him at table football.

'So,' I would say as he scored another goal, 'are you going to take *End Product*?'

'Oh, yes,' he would say, launching his next attack.

'What about *A Series of Defeats*?'

'Yes, we're taking that, too. Didn't Mike Shaw tell you?' Up to that point Mike probably had no idea they were taking the book either, but I cheerfully blamed him for not letting me know.

End Product was a futuristic story – which I had written with considerable factual input from my friend Dr John Poole, a chemist and former librarian at the House of Commons – set in South Africa at a future time of famine when white people were farming black people as food. No, I didn't put it forward as a serious concept, it was supposed to be a satire. Another friend, Ian Chapman, then managing director of William Collins, was keen to publish it, but William Collins himself turned it down as too controversial and, since he owned the firm, he had the last word. Ian tried it on him a second time but Collins was still adamant that he wouldn't have it, especially as there had been race riots in Notting Hill and other places, and by the time Quartet took it the world had moved on. Race hadn't ceased to be an issue in this country – it never has – but by then the tension had eased off and Britain had other political problems on its mind. My story was no longer topical. So when Quartet published the book it made very little impact, although I do feel that if it had come out when Ian first wanted to publish, it might have been quite sensational. Timing again, you see – the right book at the right time and bestsellerdom looms; the right book at the wrong time and forget it.

I rounded off the seventies with *The Hollywood Greats*, a book based on and expanding on the first two series of programmes I had made for the BBC.

I had begun the decade in comparative obscurity as a *Daily Mail* journalist with a couple of novels behind me, and finished it basking in modest fame as a regular national broadcaster on television and radio with seven books to my name. Who would ever have predicted that?

10

Diana Norman, Novelist

IT WOULD HARDLY be fair to say that Diana was lying dormant during the seventies. In fact, she'd probably (and quite rightly) have killed me if I'd suggested any such thing. After all, she had kind of important matters to attend to, like running the house and bringing up two young daughters. And if that wasn't enough, around the middle of the decade she also became a magistrate on the Stevenage bench, a post she accepted with the utmost reluctance. She didn't want to do it but felt she ought to, as a public duty. In fact, she disliked it so much that after a while she went to our vicar, Julian Tross, to tell him she was thinking of resigning and to ask his advice.

She didn't mind sentencing genuine rogues and scallywags, she said, but she hated fining or sending to prison destitute single mothers and the like whose crime was that they hadn't paid their television licence fee because they didn't have any money.

'I just don't enjoy it,' she said, unhappily.

'I see,' said Julian. 'So you think it's better to leave the job to those who do enjoy sending poor people to prison?'

After that she bit the bullet and continued her magistracy for seventeen years, until the birth of Emma's twins, Bertie and Oliver, in 1993.

During her time on the bench she took my mother to a hospital appointment one day. Mum was pretty frail at the time and had to be pushed in a wheelchair along the corridor to the clinic. She was also very deaf and tended to speak rather loudly, which she proceeded to do in the waiting room as she pointed out the deficiencies of the other patients to Diana, for instance: 'Look at that poor old cow over there – look at the size of her.'

Diana couldn't get her out of there fast enough and wheeled her rapidly back to the car, installed her in the passenger seat and was about to take the hospital wheelchair back to its rightful berth when Mum said: 'Hang on, Di, stick that in the boot. You can keep it in your garage. Be ideal for wheeling me along your path.'

Diana said: 'Betty, I can't do that – I'm a magistrate. I can't steal hospital property.'

My mother treated this petty quibble with the contempt she thought it deserved and was grimly silent for much of the journey home.

* * *

For a while, too, as a result of a magazine article she had written, Diana became involved with the National Society for the Prevention of Cruelty to Children, helping to arrange day trips to our village for deprived inner-city kids, most of whom had never even seen a field and thought the whole world was covered in tarmac and paving stones. On the first of these visits a cow popped its head over a hedge just as a five-year-old was wandering by. The kid looked up at it in terror. 'Bloody 'ell!' he said. 'What's that?' and ran to Diana for sanctuary.

So she wasn't exactly idle in the seventies. But apart from freelance journalism and learning all she could about Henry II, her writing career was in abeyance until the end of the decade. In 1970 she'd published *Road from Singapore*, the biography of a remarkable man named John Dodd, an RAF corporal and devout Christian who, when the Japanese invaded Singapore, escaped to Java, eluded capture for six months, spent the rest of the war in the notorious hellhole of Changi Jail and devoted himself afterwards to helping ex-convicts towards rehabilitation as the general secretary of the Langley House Trust, which provided halfway houses for people released from prison.

But after that book there was nothing until 1980, when *Fitzempress' Law* announced the arrival of Diana Norman, novelist. To a large extent it owed its existence to Bernard Levin, who, over lunch one day, was telling us about G. K. Chesterton's essay on the British jury system, 'The Twelve Men'. Diana was fascinated. 'Go and read it,' Bernard said and then, being Bernard, made sure she did by sending her a copy the next day.

Diana's book tells the story of three modern teenage delinquents who are taken back in time to the twelfth century and, of course, Henry II and the jury system. For readers of historical fiction it has now become a minor classic and used copies of it change hands for £220 upwards. Like all her books, it was exhaustively researched and the author wore her knowledge lightly. Not for her the writer's all too common ploy of saying in effect: 'Right, listen up – I'm about to tell you something you didn't know before.' No, she simply tossed in bits of recondite information and let them lie there for readers to absorb or not as they chose.

Nor did she ever write bodice-rippers. To borrow a line from that all-round man of letters Frank Muir, nowhere in her work will you find sentences like 'She felt his hot breath on her neck as he ripped the thin silk from . . .' In fact, she hated writing anything like a sex scene; she had to gear herself up for it because it embarrassed her. And she agonized deeply if one of her characters had to be killed off.

Fitzempress' Law was an immediate critical success and what thrilled Diana most was that the Irish writer Frank Delaney chose it as the best historical novel of the year on his influential Radio 4 programme *Bookshelf*, on which the historian David Starkey also gave it glowing praise.

After that she loved Starkey, whom she only met once, until she died, but then she loved everybody, particularly strangers, who complimented her on her writing. Compliments from her family she tended to ignore as merely token, though they were always genuinely sincere. We all knew how good a writer she was but she never believed us when we told her; in fact, she never truly believed she was a good writer. She once described herself as 'just a hack who got lucky', but she was far, far more than that, though she never had the self-belief to back up the obvious talent.

Whenever she was writing another novel there were many occasions when she would come stomping out of her study, scowling bitterly and saying: 'Oh, I can't do it any more. What little ability I ever had has all gone. This is the worst book I've ever written.'

And we, the family, would merely say: 'Ah, shut up. You say that every time and you're always wrong.' So she was. Each book was better than the one before.

My father was quick to recognize her gifts. 'God, she's a good writer,' he said when he read *Fitzempress' Law*. I don't recall him ever saying anything like that about my books. I think he liked them (though I believe my mother enjoyed them more and, in fact, often reread them) and he very nearly succeeded in getting Roger

Moore to star in a film version of *The Matter of Mandrake* even before it was published. Roger was keen but, alas, he was committed at the time to making several more episodes of *The Saint* for TV and that put the kibosh on the movie plans. When he next made a film he chose to play James Bond instead of my hero, Paul Baker. A seriously bad career move, if you ask me.

Dad was right: Dee was a good writer, better than me and also very different. We never read each other's work in progress because there wasn't really any point; her mind worked one way, mine another, although sometimes she would seek my advice on a plot point and once or twice I was even able to help.

After *Fitzempress' Law* there was no stopping her. Between 1980 and 2006 she wrote ten more novels under the name Diana Norman, ranging in period from the twelfth to the eighteenth century, covering such subjects as the French Revolution, Restoration London, the extraordinary seventeenth-century Irish pirate Grace O'Malley, and culminating in a trilogy (*A Catch of Consequence, Taking Liberties* and *The Sparks Fly Upwards*) featuring a heroine called Makepeace and set partly in Boston, largely in London but also in Paris, around the time of the American War of Independence and taking in the Reign of Terror in post-revolutionary France. All of them took months of dedicated research, involving numerous trips to her beloved London Library, whence she would stagger home laden with plastic bags full of works of reference. And in all her novels she would mix real and fictitious characters in a seamless blend, resolutely refusing to let the real-life characters do anything that would conflict with what was known about them and their behaviour. She wasn't just a bloody good writer, she was an honourable one.

Some of the books were also published in America, many of them were translated into foreign languages (especially German) and all were enthusiastically received in lofty publications such as *The Times Literary Supplement*, which pleased her immensely. Along the way she built up a solid fan base of devoted readers, not, alas, large enough to guarantee her a place in the best-seller lists but loyal and eager enough to keep asking when her next book was coming out. I suppose she could have kept on like this till the end, choosing a period in history that particularly interested her, finding out all there was to know about it and then weaving a story around it.

But then, early in the new millennium, everything changed, with the creation of Ariana Franklin and Adelia Aguilar.

11

Designated Driver

THE SEVENTIES ENDED on what could easily have been a tragic note. In the summer of 1979 Diana drove to the Loire Valley to do some research on Henry II. Specifically, she wanted to visit Henry's castle at Chinon and also Fontevraud, to see his and Eleanor of Aquitaine's tombs. Mamfie went with her and on a Friday just outside Le Mans they had a head-on collision with a French car. Neither of the couple in the other vehicle was injured but Diana suffered a smashed mouth and broken foot and Mamf was knocked unconscious. How the accident happened they could never remember, but they were both taken to a nearby hospital, where the medical staff wanted to keep Diana in for treatment but refused to find a bed for Mamf. She had concussion and her vision was still blurred? Big deal, let her go, they said. Under no circumstances would Diana ever have let her dazed sixteen-year-old daughter wander round a strange town looking for a bed, so she discharged herself, though I can't begin to imagine what kind of pain she was in with her damaged mouth and broken foot, and, eventually, they found a hotel. From there Diana phoned me to ask if I would come and rescue them.

When I took the call I had just got home after presenting *Going Places* on the radio and there was a big problem. My car was a soft-top MGB, virtually a two-seater. I couldn't possibly bring them back from France in that, so I phoned Roger Macdonald, seeking help. 'Well,' he said, 'Tom's got a Rover he's testing for the weekend. I expect he'll lend you that.'

Tom – Tom Boswell, the programme's resident expert on all things to do with motor cars – offered much more. When I explained the circumstances he instructed me to book a ferry to Calais, drive to his home in South London and leave my car there while he and I together set off to rescue the damsels in distress in Le Mans.

I've never been so grateful to anyone. We caught the last ferry out of Dover and drove through the rest of the night and the day – taking turns at the wheel – to collect the invalids. Diana was in very bad shape – she was in such agony that Mamf had her work cut out to stop her taking too many painkillers – and wanted to go straight home, but Tom was curious as to how she had sustained her injuries. Where was her car? he asked. By chance, Diana knew and told him. Right, he said, we'll just go and look at it. She begged him not to; all she wanted to do was curl up in the back of the Rover and rest as best she might, but he was adamant. There's something not quite right here, he said, and so we drove to the site of the wreck, where Tom discovered that Diana's seat belt had snapped during the collision. He unscrewed all of it and then we went home, where she underwent lengthy dental and medical treatment on her injuries.

Tom urged us to sue the seat-belt manufacturer but Diana wasn't keen; she just wanted to forget the whole horrendous incident. Tom, though, was insistent. Open and shut case, he said, and I believed him. He was, after all, a Cambridge engineering graduate who had done the full Rolls-Royce apprenticeship and was often used as an expert witness in court cases involving motoring accidents. And because Diana was as grateful to him as I was, she reluctantly agreed, if only to please him. After much to-ing and fro-ing the company offered us £3,000 and legal costs by way of compensation. Tom said this was risible. If we threatened to take the matter all the way to court, he said, he was confident they would cough up a lot more. Mine was by then a quite familiar name and that, plus my association with *Going Places*, which, after all, dealt with motoring matters, would guarantee newspaper coverage and the kind of publicity the company would wish to avoid. But at this point Diana resisted; she was appalled at the prospect of giving evidence in court and having to admit that she had no idea how the accident had happened. So she accepted the £3,000, much to Tom's disgust.

Still, she repaid his kindness in other ways. When, some years later, he was dying of cancer she visited him more often than I did and helped to nurse him.

I had learned to drive in Johannesburg. For my twenty-first birthday, my father, who happened to be in Jo'burg at the time, bought me my first, tailor-made, dinner jacket and put down a large deposit on a Morris Minor. I failed my first test because I'd only had eight lessons and no practice and could hardly drive at all; I failed the second because I scraped against another car and the picky examiner held that against me. On my third attempt I passed.

Diana learned to drive when we moved to Hertfordshire. She had to, really. Our house was half a mile from the village shop and the post office, both of which stocked only the necessities; the nearest butcher, grocer and greengrocer were a mile and a half away in Knebworth and there were only two bus services a day.

Sitting with her to give her practice between lessons was interesting. The first time she turned a corner with me alongside her she said: 'That was okay, wasn't it?'

'Fine,' I said, 'though perhaps best to keep off

the pavement. It does rather alarm the pedestrians.'

Another time, she was driving us to my parents' home in Edgware along the A1, before it became a dual carriageway. After a bit a grassy roundabout loomed ahead. 'Which way do I go?' she asked.

'Straight ahead,' I said, so she did. She bumped up on to the roundabout, drove across the top of it and bumped down into the road on the other side. Much swerving of cars, screeching of brakes and cursing of drivers, to say nothing of the anguished screams coming from the seat beside Diana.

'Why the hell did you do that?' I said, when all danger had passed. Never in her life could she possibly have seen anyone drive straight across a roundabout.

'Well, you told me to do it,' she said, and thus, as in every dispute between us, all blame lay firmly with me.

Soon after she got her licence there was a quiz on TV to test the audience's driving skills. Diana insisted that we should both do it and she scored one more point than I did. That – along with the fact that she had passed her test first time and I hadn't – apparently proved beyond any argument that she was and always would be a better driver than me and, from then on, she insisted on driving whenever we went out together. I didn't mind too much; it meant that when we were going to a dinner or a party I was the designated drinker. But she took it further than that; unless she had absolutely no choice, she would never let anyone else drive her, insisting that she was terrified of speed. This was a complete nonsense. She was quite the fastest driver in the family, the only one to be booked for doing 102 mph on the M5. In my car. With me, as usual, in the passenger seat. When the police had finished giving her the ticket and we were proceeding, much more sedately, on our way, she gave me a stern look. 'That's the trouble with your car,' she said. 'It goes much faster than you realize.' So that was my fault, too.

Actually, she was a good driver, though she never did get the hang of roundabouts. Time after time, we'd be going round one when the car behind would hoot furiously. 'Why's he blasting his horn at me?' she would ask, indignantly, and I would have to tell her that she had suddenly changed lanes halfway round and you really shouldn't do that on a roundabout. It didn't make any difference; she would still do it. The girls often complained about her driving, but I always felt comfortable with her at the wheel. Fatalism, I suppose. The way I saw it was that if there were to be a fatal car crash it would be far better if we both died together.

The strong possibility that such a thing might have happened came home to me one day quite late in her life, after she had had cataracts removed from both eyes. The whole family was in the car, Diana driving of course, and one of the girls said: 'How's your vision, Mum, since the operations?'

151

'Oh, wonderful,' she said. 'I can even read the road signs now.'

Not that she bothered much with road signs, not when she had a passenger aboard. On such occasions it was my belief that before starting the engine she removed her brain and sat on it, because I lost count of the times when I would say something like: 'Where are you going? We were supposed to take the M3 and you've just passed the turn-off.'

'Well, I didn't know,' she would say. 'I'm just the driver. I can't do the navigating as well.' God knows how she ever got to her destination when she was alone. Especially in the days before satnavs.

One day on a family outing, we were going along a dual carriageway when Dee, who had been eating an apple, threw the core out of the window. It went across the intersection, through the open window of a car coming the other way, hit the driver on the side of the head and bounced out into the road. The other car swerved violently, and we could see the bewildered driver rubbing his head and gazing around to see what on earth had hit him.

For what turned out to be our last family holiday, in 2009, Diana and I had decided for once not to drive down to Catalonia but to fly to Gerona with Mamfie, Emma and our three grandsons and rent cars there. At dinner with Woody – Andrew Wood, Emma's partner – and his daughter, Chloe, the night before we left, Diana had announced that of course she would be doing the driving in Spain because 'I'm the best driver, especially on the continent.' She turned to me: 'Aren't I?' she said. 'Yes,' I said, obediently.

So at Gerona Airport she hired the car and told Emma, Bertie and me to wait while she got it out of its slot in the multi-storey car park. She managed that bit all right then set off confidently in our direction and immediately proceeded to smash the rear passenger door while going the wrong way round a bollard, ripping the door handle right off.

Diana and I flew home before the end of that holiday, so Emma had to return the battered vehicle to the airport. She filled in the damage form as follows: Time car collected: 1 p.m. Time of accident: 1.05 p.m. Location of accident: Car park.

There is one more motoring story, from which, this time, I don't emerge too well. Early in 2004 the country suffered heavy snowfall, for which of course it was quite unprepared. The roads hadn't been gritted, no snow-ploughs were evident, and motorists were marooned overnight in their cars on an ice-bound M11. (Well, I ask you, who would ever expect snow in England in February?) One day when conditions were pretty much at their worst and I was in London, Diana and Emma had to pick Bertie up from his school in Letchworth. I suggested they use my car, an expensive automatic model, which appeared to have a special gear for driving in snow, rather than Diana's. That was a big mistake – mine was a rear-wheel drive, and the snow gizmo proved useless. It took them hours to get back to Datchworth, in part because once or twice on hills the car flatly refused to move and kind motorists had to push it to get it under way again. In the end they reached the outskirts of the village, where the roads were particularly slippery, manoeuvred the thing into a lay-by and gave up. Fortunately, a local family passing by squeezed them all into their car and took them the last mile home.

The next day, Diana, Emma, Bertie and I trudged through deep snow across the fields to where my car awaited us. I got into the driving seat and the others pushed to get it going. But as soon as they'd shoved the car on to the icy road it started skidding and sliding, and I knew (well, that's my story anyway) that if I stopped to let the others in I'd never get it to move again and the road would be blocked. So, to their horror, I simply drove on and was proved right when, a couple of hundred yards from home, the damn thing stopped dead and informed me that, although motionless, it was skidding. A group of women who were passing by gave it a shove, and I managed to get it home. But I'd forgotten in my anxiety to thank these women and I was walking back to do so when a neighbour, Tony Charles, drove by with Diana, Emma and Bertie on board.

I waved, only to hear Diana mutter grimly: 'Don't stop, Tony, don't stop.' And then she leaned out of the window, shaking her fist at me and yelling: 'You bastard!'

A few days later in church Tony's wife, Ann, took Emma to one side and asked with great concern: 'Is everything all right with your parents?'

Well, of course it was. By then. For a while, I have to say, Diana was not best pleased at having been abandoned and contemptuously brushed my explanation aside as unworthy of consideration. She did forgive me, though, but she never forgot – at various times thereafter when, presumably, she thought I was getting a bit above myself, she would remind me of how, selfishly, I had left her, her daughter and her grandson to make their way home in freezing conditions while I drove off in a heated car.

12

You've Got to Have a Story

FOR ME, THE EIGHTIES began well. BAFTA (the British Academy of Film and Television Arts) presented me with the Richard Dimbleby Award for a notable contribution to factual television – virtually the only award available to presenters, as opposed to actors, on TV – but then I left the film programme to write and present the BBC's flagship arts programme *Omnibus*, which had been off the air for a while but was now to be reintroduced in 1982. Not a shrewd move. The press hated it, and me, long before the show was ever seen, believing the Beeb had brought it back in an attempt to kill off Melvyn Bragg's excellent *South Bank Show* on ITV. As far as I'm aware, no such devious plot was in anyone's mind, though the BBC did schedule *Omnibus* for Sunday nights at exactly the same time as Melvyn's programme. But I'm pretty sure you could put that down to thoughtlessness or stupidity rather than malice.

The reviews were terrible and one critic, someone I'd thought till then was a friend, wrote a jeering piece in which he claimed that he'd been offered the job before me but, unlike me, had been smart enough to turn it down. This was untrue; he'd merely been offered the chance to be one of the show's regular contributors. I have never spoken to that man since. But with all this hostility around, plus the fact that while I'd been assured that *Omnibus* would take its tone from me it actually did nothing of the sort, I decided to get out as fast as possible. In my year on the programme I learned a lot about aspects of the arts of which hitherto I had been ignorant but, in effect, I'd been reduced most of the time to a mere presenter of other people's items.

Generally speaking, it was not a happy year for me, although there were a few episodes that stick in my memory – a survey of a significant British presence on Broadway, a look at fashion in Milan, and a profile of David Puttnam after *Chariots of Fire* had won several Oscars. Plus there was a tour of a Japanese exhibition in London on which I was accompanied by the former prime minister, Ted Heath, who farted silently but noisomely as we walked around.

Featured in the Brits on Broadway episode was Andrew Lloyd Webber, whose *Cats* was about to open there. We were to interview him, as I recall, on the top of the Carnegie Building, which is a hell of a long way up from the ground. When he joined my producer, Robin Lough, the crew and me up there, the first thing he said was: 'I can't possibly do anything until I've had some coffee.'

'Fine,' said Robin. 'Someone will pop down and get some for you.'

'Oh no,' said Andrew. 'We'll have to go to the café and sit down.'

So he and Robin and I took the elevator down to the ground floor and sat drinking coffee and chatting while the crew, coffeeless, waited on the roof. I thought that was inconsiderate of him, although he did give Robin and me tickets to the first night of *Cats*.

While I was doing all these things, Barry Brown, as producer of the film programme, had tried out several people in my absence – the actress Maria Aitken; Tina Brown, who went on to a distinguished journalistic and social career in New York and is the wife of Sir Harry Evans, former editor of *The Times*; Miles Kington, a clever humorous columnist for *Punch*, among other publications; and the broadcaster Glyn Worsnip, each of whom had a three-month stint on the show.

Clive James, who, for reasons I've never understood, rather objected to my being given the Dimbleby Award – something for which Diana never forgave him – was much taken with Tina Brown and in his TV review in the *Observer* conjured up an image of me returning to the show to present it with her and sitting, purring contentedly, in her lap. I rather think he really had visions of himself purring contentedly in her lap, but there you go. Glyn Worsnip somewhat screwed up his opportunity by borrowing and closely studying some of my scripts for the film programme and deciding from them that it was simply a matter of making jokes about the movies. He couldn't have been more wrong; I liked making jokes, but only about bad films – the others I tried to treat seriously (though never, I hope, solemnly). Miles Kington was easily the best of the four but, luckily for me, he wasn't that interested in being on television, otherwise I think he would have been offered the job full-time. As it was, when I said I would be leaving *Omnibus* at the end of the year, Barry Brown immediately asked me to come back to the film show and I was very happy to agree.

My return to *Film '83*, of course, revived my professional connection with the movie industry, which had really begun on the *Daily Mail* some twenty years earlier and involved me in a number of occasionally bizarre encounters ...

Around 1961, I had my first meeting with Stanley Kubrick, who with his producer, James Harris, was then making *Lolita*. The three of us met one afternoon in the bar of a West End hotel, where they sat on tall bar stools, and because they were both rather short, their feet didn't reach the ground. In the brief item I wrote about them for the *Mail*'s gossip column I casually mentioned this fact.

I didn't see either of them again until at least ten years later when I was at a film reception at another West End hotel, where a publicity woman said: 'Barry, I must introduce you to Stanley Kubrick.' And Kubrick, who was standing beside her, said with a stony face: 'I remember you. You wrote that article about me and James Harris and our feet not reaching the ground. Very funny.' Then he walked away, leaving me feeling slightly chilled. I mean, God, if he could still coldly remember something as trivial as that after all this time . . .

My final contact with him, however, was much more pleasant. In 1987, Kubrick made his Vietnam War movie *Full Metal Jacket* and his publicity man phoned me to ask whether I'd seen it yet and if so what I thought of it, 'because Stanley wants to know'. This was very flattering. In fact, I had seen it and liked it a great deal and said so on my programme.

The following Sunday evening the PR man called again when I was at home watching telly. 'Sorry to disturb you, Sunday evening and all that. Are you busy?' I said I wasn't. 'Fine, then have you got time to talk to Stanley?' I said I had and Kubrick came on the line to thank me for my review of his film. This was highly unusual. Directors, producers and the like would often phone me – well, not me, but my producer – to complain bitterly if I'd hated their work, but hardly anyone ever thanked me for a friendly review.

After we'd discussed *Full Metal Jacket* for a while I said: 'What are you doing next, Stanley?' and he said: 'I don't know. What do you suggest?' Flabbergasted, I said: 'Me? ME? Come on, you must have a million ideas.'

And then, with genuine horror in his voice, he said something that was both self-evident and profound. 'No, no! You can't make a film on an idea – you've got to have a story.'

That is something that should be printed in huge capital letters and plastered on to the office walls of every film-maker in the world, because too many of them are content to make 'high concept' movies, which is to say movies that are based only on an idea, which run out of steam about halfway through and can only be resolved by winding things up with an illogical battle, explosion, high-speed chase or gunfight.

They should learn from Kubrick, who knew what he was talking about: You can't make a film on an idea.

Also in 1961, I was invited by Twentieth Century Fox to cover the filming of Darryl Zanuck's D-Day movie, *The Longest Day*, which was on location on the Ile de Ré, just off La Rochelle. 'We'll fly you to Paris,' I was told, 'but then you'll have to go by train to La Rochelle with a bunch of actors. Is that okay?'

'Yes,' I said. 'I don't mind mixing with actors, so long as none of my friends finds out.'

I met the actors at the Paris railway station. Two of them, Michael Medwin and Norman Rossington, I knew already; the third, a big, bald Scotsman in sweater and jeans, I'd neither met nor heard of. He introduced himself as Sean Connery and, somehow, as the crowded train pulled out – for reasons I never understood, everyone seemed to be going to La Rochelle that day – he and I found ourselves sitting on the floor of a third-class compartment. Medwin, always a sharp customer, had found first-class seats for himself and Rossington.

After a bit I asked Connery (who only had a cough and a spit in *The Longest Day*) what he was doing next. 'Och,' he said. 'Ah'm playing Jamesh Bawnd.' He didn't sound at all happy about it and I wondered, sympathetically, whether things were tough. 'Well, it'sh a jawb,' he said. The next time I met him, at the Paris premiere of *Dr No*, he had become a superstar virtually overnight, although the French television commentators found his name embarrassing to mention, quite understandably, because in French 'connerie' means at its politest 'damn stupidity'. Still, as we know, it doesn't seem to have held him back.

In the late sixties, Connery decided he'd had enough of playing James Bond and, the franchise by now being well established, there was much speculation about who would take over. So I went to Harry Saltzman, who then co-produced the films with Cubby Broccoli. 'Who's it to be?' I asked.

'We're still looking,' he said. 'Any ideas?'

'Well, I'm free,' I said. 'Look no further.' I rather fancied the idea. All right, I'd never done any acting, but I was young, pretty fit and though not as sexy as Connery I certainly had more hair than he did. Besides, I was pretty sure that playing James Bond would pay better than journalism. But Saltzman just laughed, which I thought was very rude.

And who did he end up with? George Lazenby. Served him right. I still reckon I could have done better. Lazenby's only appearance as Bond was in *On Her Majesty's Secret Service*, in which his co-star was Diana Rigg. The story goes that they didn't get on at all well, to such an extent that whenever they had to play a love scene the next day, she made sure she ate something liberally laced with garlic that evening. I've no idea whether this is true or not but somehow I like to think it is. I also like to think that, had I been playing Bond, Diana, who once stood guard for me outside a ladies' loo when I was desperate for a pee, wouldn't have eaten the garlic.

In 1978, I was on the Bond movie location in Rio de Janeiro, where they were filming *Moonraker*. One morning on Sugar Loaf Mountain, I was about to interview the then-current Bond, Roger Moore, when Cubby Broccoli took me to one side. It was well known at the time that he and Roger were at loggerheads, Cubby wanting him to sign for the next in the series and Roger saying he would only do it for more money.

'Ask him,' said Cubby. 'Ask him if he's going to do the next movie.'

I liked Cubby and knew him quite well, but I'd known Roger a lot longer, so I warned him that the question was coming. I was sure he'd be equal to it; Roger is an absolute master of the charming but bland and utterly non-committal answer to any difficult question, and he duly came up with just such an answer. Somehow, without committing himself in any way, he gave the impression that he might make the next film but on the other hand he might not.

The interview over, Cubby pulled me to one side. 'Well,' he said, 'what did that asshole of an actor have to say?'

I told him what the asshole of an actor had had to say and Cubby said, 'Oh, fuck!' and stomped away. They did resolve matters in the end, though, and I daresay Roger was able to up his fee considerably.

I met Brigitte Bardot twice in 1967, when she was quite the sexiest creature the movies had ever known. She was to come to London for location shooting on her film

Two Weeks in September and the *Mail* had the bright idea of sending me to Paris to interview her before she got here. Her agent was willing, so was Bardot, but when I turned up there was a snag: urgent retakes were necessary on whatever movie she was just completing and, ah, *quel dommage*, she simply didn't have time to see me. I hung around Paris hopefully for a few days (no great hardship) and then the agent came up with a solution: what if Brigitte and I flew to London together and I did the interview on the plane? Great idea, although as I sauntered into the crowded first-class compartment side by side with every man's sexual fantasy I was the recipient of the most vitriolic looks of pure envy and hatred imaginable from all the goggle-eyed businessmen around us.

A few days later I met Bardot again. She was doing some filming in North London and the press turned out in force. Unfortunately, it started to rain quite heavily and the shooting was called off. We journalists crowded around her, each trying to get as close as possible to this infinitely desirable young woman.

'*Alors*,' purred the Sex Kitten, 'what shall we do now? I know – let's go back to my hotel and play poker.'

We stared at each other, open-mouthed. Play poker with Brigitte Bardot? In her hotel room? Wow!

And then – I still can't believe it – every one of us said no. Love to, we said, really love to, but, you know, dead-lines and all that, got to get back to the office, what a terrible shame . . . And we all slunk off. What a bunch of wimps. Afterwards, of course, we tried to justify ourselves with macho bravado. If she'd said 'strip poker', we agreed, well, that would have been very different, oh yes indeed.

But we knew it was a lie. The fact is that when push came to shove even the most randy of us simply had no idea how to cope with so much feminine sexuality close up and we just chickened out. I regret it to this day.

In the late sixties, I had an odd experience in Hong Kong. Among other things, I was there to interview a very famous British movie star. He was agreeable and, at his invitation, one afternoon I went to his hotel suite, where I found him and his young – and no doubt temporary – American mistress. They were both wearing fluffy white hotel bathrobes and, it seemed pretty obvious, nothing else. It also seemed pretty obvious what they'd been up to before I arrived. I was surprised, because I knew he was married with a family, which is why I'm not going to identify him. I've no idea whether his wife and children were aware of his extramarital activities, but I have to assume they weren't and I don't wish to hurt them. So I'll just call him John, though that wasn't his real name.

He introduced me to the girl, and then he and I sat and talked while she poured us drinks. Just before I left, John invited me to join him and his girlfriend at dinner that night; they were being entertained by a group of wealthy Chinese and he assured me I'd be welcome, so I accepted.

Looking back, what strikes me as remarkable about that meeting is that nothing like it could possibly happen now. With an international press and readership, to say nothing of the Internet, seizing voraciously on the misbehaviour of the famous, no movie star today would welcome a journalist into his hotel suite when he'd just got out of bed with his mistress. But in the sixties, I (and I'm sure many other journalists) had relationships with such people that were based on mutual trust. We had an unspoken agreement that there were certain things I wouldn't write about and, in return, I was given off-the-record information that would prove invaluable in the future. So I was quite pleased that John, whom I hardly knew, had trusted me.

Well, I thought he had, but later that evening it became clear that he was having his doubts. Midway through dinner, where I was the only unescorted guest, I saw John whispering urgently to our host, who looked across at me, nodded, then summoned an underling and whispered things to him.

A few minutes later the underling returned with a very pretty Chinese girl, dressed attractively though much less expensively than the other women present, for whom room was found beside me at the table. She smiled at me, I smiled back and said something, and she looked baffled. It was pretty obvious that her grasp of English was modest at best, and my Cantonese was non-existent.

John got up and came over to me. 'She's very pretty, isn't she?' he murmured into my ear. I agreed she was. He patted me on the shoulder. 'Have a nice evening,' he said. 'Everything's settled,' and then he went back to his chair and grinned encouragingly at me.

So that was how much he trusted me: just enough to fix me up with a prostitute, so that I would be as compromised as he was. If I blew the whistle on him, he could do the same for me.

I stayed long enough to enjoy the meal, then, as the liqueurs were being ordered, I thanked my host, said goodbye to John and his mistress, shook hands with the silent girl beside me and thanked her for her company and went back to my hotel. Alone.

Any respect I'd had for John vanished after that, not because of his philandering – that was none of my business – but because he'd tried to buy me off with a hooker.

I'm going to boast a bit now. One year, we rounded off the film programme's season by doing the show from New York before going off for our summer break. We did that quite often but, this time, unusually, we decided to record the whole programme in Manhattan rather than bring the material home and put it together here. To this end, Barry Brown, then my producer, hired a studio and crew for a day and we turned up in the morning to rehearse. This went very well and, after lunch, we returned to record the show.

We did it as if it were live. I didn't fluff once, all the clips came in smoothly on time and twenty-nine minutes and thirty seconds after we started it was all over. When Barry said: 'Thank you, everyone, that's a wrap,' there was a moment's silence on the studio floor and then, led by the floor manager, the whole crew gave Barry and me an ovation.

I thought they were taking the mickey and said so. 'Jeez, no,' said the floor manager. 'I mean, is that really how you guys do television over there – straight through like that?'

I said that was how we always tried to do it, and he said: 'Oh, my God – how can I get a job with the BBC? We had a guy in here the other day to do a thirty-second commercial. It took him two hours, and you guys did thirty minutes straight through.'

Barry and I were very proud of that.

The only person I have ever met who was to be charged with murder was O. J. Simpson. It was in Basle, where they were filming *Cassandra Crossing*, a thriller starring Richard Harris and Sophia Loren, in 1975. At that time Simpson was still combining his day job as a huge American football star for the Buffalo Bills with a nascent film career, and he had a small part in the movie. He had never been to Switzerland before and I asked him how he was enjoying it.

'Great,' he said. 'In the States people come up to me everywhere. Here I can walk down the street and nobody knows who I am.'

A couple of days later I bumped into him again when he was looking much less cheerful and asked how things were going. 'Awful,' he said. 'I hate this place. I walk down the street and nobody knows who I am.'

Twenty years later, after a lengthy and controversial trial at which he was cleared of the murder of his ex-wife Nicole and her friend Ronald Goldman, even people who disliked films and American football knew who he was. (In a subsequent civil trial he was found liable for the death of Goldman and the battery of Nicole.)

One of my tasks as the BBC's film reviewer was to cover the Oscars. One year, a few days before the ceremony I was in my Beverly Hills hotel room, dutifully swotting up on the stuff I should have at my fingertips for the big event, when Valerie, my sister, who was living in the San Fernando Valley, phoned me.

'Do you know Mel Gibson?' she said.

'No, I'm sorry, Val, I don't,' I said. 'I like his work but I'm afraid I've never met him.' (This was at a time when he was still best known as a big movie star and hadn't acquired his more recent reputation as a drink-driving anti-Semite.)

'Oh, that's all right,' she said. 'He's coming to dinner at our house tomorrow night. Why don't you join us, and I'll introduce you.'

The reason Gibson was having dinner at my sister's house was that she was then still married to Bernie Williams, who had produced *The Bounty*, in which Gibson played Fletcher Christian to Anthony Hopkins' Captain Bligh, and they'd become good friends.

The other guests that evening were Roger Donaldson, director of *The Bounty*, and his wife, also named Mel, and the cinematographer John Alcott and his wife, Sue. I'd never met any of them before but they all greeted me warmly – all, that is, except Gibson, who was decidedly cool towards me. I was a bit surprised. I didn't necessarily expect him to love me at first sight but he had quite clearly taken against me. All I got from him was a brief handshake and a curt 'How d'you do?' before he turned his back on me and carried on talking to Val and Bernie. So I chatted to the Donaldsons and the Alcotts, who were very nice, and then Gibson suddenly turned towards me.

'How tall are you?' he asked.

'Just over six foot.'

'No, you're not,' he said.

'Well, I am as a matter of fact.'

'No, you're not – you're no taller than me.' He was

about five foot eight or nine. So I said: 'Well, I think I am taller than you.'

'No, you're not.' Now this would have been quite amusing except that he seemed deadly serious, almost angry, and the atmosphere was becoming rather unpleasant until some tactful person said: 'I know – why don't you two stand back to back and then we can see who's the taller.'

'Okay,' I said, 'fine.'

So we stood back to back and I could feel him going up on tiptoe behind me so that the top of his head would reach the same level as mine and then the tactful person said: 'There you are – you're exactly the same height.'

And Gibson turned to me and said: 'See, I told you so.'

I looked down at him and shrugged. 'Okay, Mel, if you're happy, I'm happy.' But what the hell was that all about? Maybe I missed the joke but why should it matter to him that someone he'd never met before might be a few inches taller than he was? I dunno. Movie stars. What can you do with them?

To be fair, some of them are likeable, level-headed people, but others are much less so. Many of them seem to have a firm policy that if you are to do an interview with them you must be kept waiting, and I don't mean just for a few minutes, I mean for anything up to an hour and a half. I truly believe this stems from a lack of self-confidence, to prove to themselves as much as you that they are more important than you are. I had no problem with that notion, but I'd have been a lot happier if they'd turned up on time, taken me to one side and said: 'Look, let's get this straight – I'm more important than you are.' To which I would have replied: 'Fine, now can we get on with the interview?'

But because this deliberate lateness was so prevalent I knew exactly what to expect when I first met George Clooney. The interview, at the Warner Brothers studio in Burbank, was to take place just before *Batman and Robin* opened. Nobody, including me, had seen the movie, but everyone was very excited about it because it was clearly bound to catapult Clooney from TV heart-throb in *ER* to A-list movie star. As it turned out, the film was so bad that it killed off the Batman franchise for several years and almost ended Clooney's movie career before it had really started, but, of course, we didn't know that yet.

My crew and I turned up in plenty of time and got ourselves set up. About ten minutes before Clooney was due to arrive I said I had to go to the loo. My producer, Bruce Thompson, and the crew were horrified. 'You can't,' they said.

'Why not?'

'Well, the lavatory's right down the end of that corridor and he'll be here any minute.'

'No, he won't,' I said. 'He'll be late. They're always late. You know that perfectly well. Besides, I simply have to pee.'

So off I went and when I'd done my stuff and re-emerged into the long corridor I looked up and saw Clooney chatting to my crew. Not only had he turned up early, which was almost unheard of, he had come alone, which was even more unheard of. Usually the stars arrived surrounded by agents, managers, press agents and sometimes bodyguards. I hurried towards him, arm outstretched in greeting. 'Good to see you,' I said.

He looked at me suspiciously. 'Have you washed your hands?' he asked, and right away I knew that we'd get along fine, as indeed we did.

I liked him even more at the end of the interview when Liz Ekberg, our very pretty director, who like many women was somewhat smitten with Clooney, asked if she could have her photograph taken with him.

'You know, George,' I said crassly, 'what she would really have liked was to sit on your lap throughout the interview.'

Clooney looked at me, then at Liz. 'Shall I hit him for you now?' he asked her.

The 1996 Oscars were a triumph for Mel Gibson. He won the award for best director for *Braveheart*, in which he also starred as William Wallace, who in 1305 led the

Scots in battle against King Edward I. After the ceremony he turned up in somewhat disgruntled mood for the post-Oscars party thrown by *Vanity Fair* at Morton's restaurant in Beverly Hills. The reason for his disgruntlement was a kilted bagpiper walking along a few yards behind him and blowing lustily into his pipes.

'What's he doing here?' I asked.

'Oh God,' Gibson said, 'he's been following me around all day. It was Jodie Foster's idea – she hired him. Didn't tell me. But he's been following me everywhere. I can't shake him off.'

He did shake him off at Morton's, though. Only stars were invited and the bagpiper certainly wasn't a star so they wouldn't let him in.

I didn't enjoy the Oscars, not because I never attended the actual ceremony – the only television company allowed into that was ABC, which covered it live – but because for the first several years what it entailed for me was this: watch the show over a snack dinner in hotel room; change swiftly into dinner jacket, then go to Morton's restaurant and stand outside in line with about a hundred other TV outfits and hope the stars, on their way in, would deign to stop and talk to us.

Even as a young reporter I had always hated doorstepping people, and I found it no less demeaning in such supposedly glamorous circumstances as these. Besides, by now it was getting on for midnight and often very cold (the nights are not warm in Los Angeles in the early part of the year) and sometimes it drizzled.

The stars, the nominees and winners would draw up in their stretch limos to be greeted by a hundred television crews yelling their names and demanding their attention. (I flatly refused to join in the yelling and my producer, Bruce Thompson, gallantly did it for me.) The stars would then wander across and stroll down the line deigning to give the interviewers soundbites before going into the restaurant to stuff their faces, leaving us shivering outside.

And, for me, it didn't get any better when in the last few years of my time at the BBC we took the show live. This meant my sitting in a tiny rented studio somewhere in Hollywood and filling in the numerous commercial breaks on American TV by chatting to the odd guest about what we had just seen and what to expect. The first time we did this I thought, Well, at least I won't have to stand outside bloody Morton's this year; I mean, three and a half hours of concentration and talk in a sweaty studio – isn't that enough?

Apparently it wasn't. 'No,' said Bruce, 'you've got to do the interviews as well. The stars know you, they don't know us; they'll talk to you but they won't talk to us.' I hummed and hawed and sulked but, eventually, I had to give in. I'm afraid there were times when poor Bruce Thompson and Liz Ekberg had to put up with a lot of bad behaviour from me.

There was just one occasion outside Morton's that I remember with mild satisfaction and that was only because it gave me an ego boost. I was standing in line alongside a very pretty girl from LA's Channel 7, which admittedly made the situation more pleasant than usual, when Anthony Hopkins, at the peak of his fame as Hannibal Lecter, got out of his car and walked briskly towards the restaurant, clearly not wanting to talk to anyone and ignoring the frenzied shouts of 'Sir An-tho-ny! Sir An-tho-ny!'

Then Bruce spotted him. 'Oi, Tony!' he yelled. 'Come over here and talk to Barry!' And Tony stopped, waved and came across and, having spoken to me, clearly felt obliged to speak to a few others as well. When he had gone the girl from Channel 7 gazed at me with something approaching awe. 'You must be very famous,' she said. And the guy beside her and the guy beside me said much the same thing. I just smiled. Modestly, of course.

I remember one other occasion when Bruce used the same tactic. It was the night *Titanic* undeservedly won all those Oscars and Rupert Murdoch, whose company Twentieth Century Fox had largely financed the film, turned up at the restaurant where the celebration party was being held.

'Do you want to talk to him?' asked Bruce.

'Might as well,' I said, so Bruce did his stuff. 'Oi, Rupert!' he hollered. 'Come over here and talk to Barry!'

To my surprise, he did, and was in fact very amiable. But I do wonder whether Bruce would have summoned Rupert Murdoch in quite such a peremptory fashion had he known that within a year both he and I would be working for him.

13

Bye Bye, Beeb

A LITTLE AFTER I had joined BSkyB I gave a talk at a public school, where one of the sixth-formers asked me sternly why I had 'betrayed' the BBC by leaving it. Actually, I don't think I did betray the BBC; if there was any betrayal at all it was more on their side than mine.

Under the director-generalship of John (now Lord) Birt, the Beeb had changed. His brief, I believe, had been to tighten the ship and cut down on excessive expenditure, and I'm sure he did that, but his methods had left those who worked there worried, unhappy and anxious. All these years later the mood still seems to be much the same; I meet very few people from the BBC who admit to being happy in their work and that's sad, because for nearly all the time I was there the Beeb was a secure and confident place, the place where everyone wanted to be.

In the summer of 1998 my contract was up for renewal and while Sue Freathy conducted her negotiations with the money people my producer Bruce Thompson went to see Peter Salmon, the fairly recently appointed controller of BBC1, to discuss the next year or so. Bruce suggested that as 1999 would end the millennium I should finish it not with my customary round-up of the best films of the year but with a look at the best films of the century.

Salmon liked this but then came up with a proposal that, when it was put to me, I did not like at all: I should do the weekly programme as usual until mid-June 1999, then come off the air for the summer and, instead of returning every week from early September, spend the rest of the year putting together the *Films of the Century* programme. In other words, from June onwards, there would be no *Film '99*, at least not with me presenting it. It was a daft idea, anyway; nobody needed several months to compile a single programme about the best films of the twentieth century, as Bruce, Liz, the rest of the team and I proved when we did exactly that at Sky while also turning out the weekly show.

What lay behind it, I suspect, was a desire to replace me as the regular film critic with someone younger. I was pushing sixty-five and the BBC seemed to have bought into the idea that what the Corporation really needed was a youthful audience with youthful presenters to attract it. In fact, it didn't then and doesn't now. Unlike all the other TV companies, it doesn't carry advertising and therefore shouldn't give a stuff what age its audience is and how much money it has to spend. I don't think it fully appreciates that out there is the biggest potential middle-aged to elderly audience television has ever had and if it simply catered to them it would attract bigger ratings than any other station in the land, thus amply justifying any anxious pleas for a higher licence fee. I don't mean it should make only programmes about the middle-aged and elderly but that it should focus on treating its audience as intelligent beings – as I had done throughout my career – and should give it stuff that required the use of the mind rather than imitating whatever lightweight material happened to be trendy and popular on other channels at that moment. Of course it treats its audience as intelligent human beings sometimes and it should regard the 'yoof' audience and its interests as important, but I don't think it should be obsessed by the latter. Anyway, if the appropriate enquiries had been made, they would quickly have learned that, on the evidence of the correspondence we received, the film programme's audience already consisted to a very large extent of sixth-formers and university undergraduates, exactly the kind of intelligent 'yoof' the BBC seemed to want.

I discussed Salmon's suggestion with Sue, who had

already agreed an acceptable sum for my next contract, and neither of us liked it at all. By the way, just in case you think I must be very rich because I was on television for a long time, let me assure you that I am not. I have no complaints about the money the BBC paid me; it was good, but it was also nothing like the Monopoly money – millions of pounds a year – that the Corporation has recently been doling out to its prize personnel. The only regret I have about my entire television career is that it ended a few years before the upper echelons at the Beeb decided, for reasons best known to themselves, that the executives and presenters should be rewarded as liberally as some bankers.

Anyway, I decided not to accept the BBC's offer but, while I was wondering how I would organize my life and my income without regular TV, BSkyB were in negotiation with Sue. They had previously approached her a couple of times enquiring about my availability and now they came up with an offer I felt I couldn't refuse. No, it wasn't just the money. 'How,' asked my indignant journalist friends, 'could you take Murdoch's shilling?' Well, it was a lot more than a shilling; it was a lot more, in fact, than the BBC had come up with, but it was the rest of the deal that tipped the balance. Rupert Murdoch's daughter, Liz, who ran the Sky film programmes, had taken the trouble to find out what interested me besides movies and produced the kind of package that had never been offered in a BBC deal: a car of my choice, a clothing allowance, season tickets to whichever Premiership football club I fancied and tickets to any Test match taking place in England. I suspect that if Sue had asked the BBC for any of those things they'd have patted her on the head and told her not to be a silly girl.

Weeks before I finally agreed to go to Sky, Sue had told the BBC that I didn't like the programme ideas they had proposed and that another television company was interested. They ignored her. Maybe they thought it was a bluff, although neither Sue nor I had ever tried to bluff them before. Or, just as likely, maybe they simply didn't care. Whatever, it was only on the day when, over lunch, Liz Murdoch and I had shaken hands on the deal that Alan Yentob, then the BBC's Director of Television, contacted me and said he wanted to talk to me urgently. We met in a hotel bar and he asked me to stay with the Corporation. I told him it was too late, that I'd given my word and wasn't going back on it.

Between that evening and my contract expiring several weeks later in mid-June, no executive of the BBC either talked to or communicated with me. From Peter Salmon, not a word. On the evening I recorded my final programme Bruce Thompson arranged a drinks and nibbles party, a sweet-sad occasion, because quite a few people seemed to have enjoyed working with me, as I had enjoyed working with them.

And that was it. I'd spent twenty-six years with the BBC, admittedly as a freelance, not a member of the staff, and I don't think I did a bad job for them. A brief note of thanks and perhaps good wishes for the future from the director-general or one of his minions would not have gone amiss; even a 'Piss off and good riddance' would at least have been an acknowledgement that I'd been around and was now leaving, but there was nothing like that. Who knows why things ended as they did? Maybe it would have been different if I had left at a time that was convenient for the BBC rather than for me. I don't think my going when I did was convenient for them as it took them the best part of a year to find a replacement for me on the film programme, my friend Jonathan Ross. (Incidentally, Jonathan and I are vaguely related by marriage. His sister Lisa is married to my nephew Matthew, Rick's younger son.)

Diana, ever protective of me, was livid on my behalf at the apparent display of indifference shown by the BBC top brass. I was not; if anything, I was wryly amused. It is rarely the case that big business – and the BBC is very big business – cares for the individual and, anyway, it could well be that I was ignored by some while I was working out my notice because they were rather worried about their own jobs. Looking at the often dumbed-down quality of the BBC – along with the rest of television in this country – over the last decade or so, maybe some of them should have been. But if they were, they, unlike me, toed the line and are still there. Do I envy them? No, I can honestly say, hand on heart, that I do not. I was deeply proud to have worked for the BBC when it was universally regarded as the best television outfit in the world, but that was then and this is now.

To go back to where this chapter started, though, did I betray the BBC as the sixth-former thought? No, I really don't think I did.

14

A Home from Home

THE FAMILY CHANGED dramatically during the nineties. Both my parents died; so did Aeron. And the three grandsons were born.

Dad died on a Friday a few weeks before his eighty-second birthday. He had been to the local surgery to pick up a prescription and was driving to the chemist to get it filled when he had a heart attack, pulled in carefully to the side of the road and died, causing a tail-back of traffic that extended almost to Stevenage. He'd have liked that.

I wrote an obituary of him for that Sunday's *Observer* and, at Bruce's request, a tribute for my film pro-gramme on the following Monday. That was very hard to do and would have been impossible for me had I known what Bruce was up to. He illustrated what I was saying about Dad with pictures of him but, being one of the most sensitive men I know, didn't tell me and didn't use them during the rehearsal. The first I knew about it was when the recording was over. If I had seen those photographs earlier I wouldn't have been able to continue.

Emma's twins, Bertie and Oliver, were born in 1993 on 5 November, which of course is the sole reason why fireworks are let off all over the land on that day. They were extremely premature and Oliver, who was born weighing 1lb 10oz – less than the proverbial bag of sugar – was never able to leave hospital and died six months later. I was with Emma on the dreadful day when the doctors at Addenbrooke's Hospital told her there was really nothing more they could do and the time had come to shut down the life support. I can't imagine how devastated Emma felt but it was one of the worst days of my life.

Bertie, who weighed 2oz more than his brother, struggled to survive, although now you wouldn't know there had ever been anything wrong with him. For much of his early life, however, he suffered badly from asthma and epilepsy, though thankfully the latter was cured by an operation at Great Ormond Street Hospital when he was six. But a few years before that, when he was less than two, he had caused us all the most enormous panic. He and Emma, along with Mamf and her husband, Piers Clifford, a cardiologist whom she had married in 1988 – wedding at Datchworth church, nice reception in a neighbouring village, great speech by the bride's father, of course – had gone to spend a few days in a house on the Seine owned by Diana's brother Tony.

While they were there Bertie developed serious bronchial problems. The local doctor was very worried about him and suggested they should get him to a hospital. Originally, they planned to drive him home and take him to hospital in Stevenage. But as they drove towards the French coast his condition worsened and they felt they had to do something immediately. They found a hospital in Rouen, where the medical staff took one look at Bertie and rushed him off for treatment before they even knew who he was.

Emma called Diana to break the news – I was at work – and she immediately got into her car and headed for France.

That evening I went down the road to see Aeron and found her lying on her chaise longue and nursing her customary cigarette and gin and tonic. She was rather given to complaining that gin wasn't nearly as strong as it used to be. What she didn't know was that Diana, a little worried about her mother's alcohol consumption (which wasn't actually all that great), had taken secretly to pouring away some of the gin and topping it up with water. Aeron was, naturally, anxious about Bertie but in good form and we chatted away for an hour or so until I went home to bed.

The next morning I phoned to check up on her. No reply. A little later I phoned again. Still no reply. By now somewhat concerned, I went to her house and knocked on the door. Nothing. I let myself in and found her looking quite peaceful in bed. She had died some time during the night – so far as I could tell without pain.

I phoned the hotel where the girls and Piers were staying and told them the news. Diana hadn't arrived yet. When she did she saw them coming down the stairs towards the foyer and knew at once from their expressions that something awful had happened. As she told me later: 'My first thought was, Oh, my God, Bertie's dead.' And then, she said, when the situation was explained she felt a confused mixture of emotions – grief that her mother had died, relief that it was her rather than Bertie. So mixed in with the relief was guilt that she should have felt it. Diana and Aeron were always very close, though they quarrelled frequently and fiercely, for they were both forceful characters. I used to call Aeron 'the Ayatollah' – with great affection, I should add, although her daughter was no less formidable an adversary. Once, Aeron was writing a letter to Emma at university when Diana drove up to take her shopping. The letter ended: 'I'll have to close now. She Who Must Be Obeyed is outside beeping.' But then, Diana and I quarrelled; so did Diana and the girls. Sometimes we even disliked each other but, as sportsmen say about form and class, like and dislike are temporary, love is permanent.

My mother died, aged close on ninety-one, a week or so before Christmas 1998. In a way it was a relief, especially, I think, for her. She had not really been happy since my father's death and in her later years had become too frail to live alone, which was a problem. She was a fiercely independent woman, who would have hated living with either Diana and me or Rick and Christine. So we found a nursing home for her, only a mile or so from both our houses, a nice, comfortable place where somebody from the family would visit her every day. But she didn't like it there and kept saying she wanted to go home, which was impossible, unless we provided carers 24/7. We'd have done that, but she would have hated the carers, too. The very idea of someone telling her what to do in her own house she would have found intolerable. So the nursing home seemed the best option. But I don't know. I still feel guilt that she died alone, in a place she didn't like, a few hours after Diana and I had visited her. I was sixty-five and lucky to have had my parents as long as I did, but I still miss them both. People say you get over their loss, but if you'd been as close as we were, you don't really; you accept it, of course, but there are still times when I wish I could seek their advice or pop in, as I often did, for a cup of tea. It wasn't that I was dependent on them, I had made my own way since I was nineteen and went to South Africa, but they were among the very few people I knew I could rely on for uncritical love and support and their absence leaves a gap that nobody else can fill.

Emma never married; Mamfie's marriage sadly ended in divorce, but not before Harry was born in 1995 and Charlie two years later. So as the decade ended the family was the same size as it was in the beginning but the personnel had changed rather dramatically.

From the mid-seventies onwards, we would holiday every year in the same place, the Catalan village of Sant Martí d'Empúries on the Mediterranean coast. Diana had found it in an advertisement in the *Sunday Times* and rather fancied it. Back then it was, just as the advertisement said, primitive but charming. Unlike the rest of the Costa Brava, it had no high-rise hotels or cafés offering 'Tea like mother make'. A few miles in either direction were resorts catering for the usual Costa Brava lager louts – all tattoos and beer bellies (and that was just the grannies) – but Sant Martí, which had been established by Julius Caesar as a retirement home for his veteran legionaries, sits beside a significant Greco-Roman archaeological site and is thus a protected village. When we first went there it was called San Martin d'Ampurias, because Franco still ruled Spain and Catalan was a forbidden language. With a mixture of pride and anger the locals would point out the bullet holes in the church, a legacy of the Spanish Civil War. As soon as Franco died all the Spanish signs were immediately replaced by their Catalan equivalents.

There were various reasons why we kept going back. Obviously, we liked the place and the people but beyond that we discovered on our second visit that my mate Ron Atkin owned a villa there, and Mamf and Emma and Ron's sons, Tim and Mike, being about the same age, swiftly became good friends. But then, too, a variety of families from France, Germany, Belgium and Holland – also with children around the girls' age – would turn up at the same time every year and, somehow, speaking only bits of each other's languages, the kids all got along famously. In particular, there was an extended German family, headed by Siegfried and Hanna, Werner and Rosemary, against whom the Normans and the Atkins would reprise the 1966 World Cup final on the beach every day. The Germans nearly always won, partly because in goal they had a grandfather who used a muumuu to stop the ball but also because, in Hanna, small and attractive though she was, they had a midfield defender as ruthless as anyone in the Premiership. The games invariably ended with handshakes all round, everyone taking a dip in the communal bath (aka the Mediterranean), bottles of wine and Coke being produced from coolers and Siegfried cooking up a mass of prawns on the beach. And that was before we all went off for lunch.

One year, a group from Birmingham – Mike and Anne, Terry and Joan, Alan and Beverley, along with their children – pitched up, too, and the Normans and the Atkins joined them for nights of eating, drinking and generally roistering in the village square. The following year another Brummie family – Roger and Sandra Partridge and their son, Adam – came, too. Roger had clearly decided he wasn't going to like the Normans – hoity-toity bloke on telly, novelist wife: what was there to like? So for a few days he barely talked to us. But one morning Emma came upon him sitting alone in the square and reading the *Sun*. 'Oh, Rog,' she said, 'can I read that when you've finished with it?'

Suddenly his attitude changed. Daughter who reads the *Sun*, I imagine he thought, family can't be all bad. Before the morning was over he and Emma had agreed to write a pornographic novel together and, though that never came to pass, the Partridges became lifelong friends and Roger is one of Bertie's godfathers.

One other reason for going to the same place every year, unadventurous though it might seem, is that as soon as you arrive you're on holiday. You know where everything is, you know where to eat and where to shop. Home from home.

Throughout their university days (University of East Anglia for both of them) and after, the girls continued to come with Diana and me to Sant Martí, not because they were in any way tied to their parents' apron strings but to renew annual acquaintance with a polyglot group of friends they'd known since childhood. We graduated from renting apartments in the village to villas just outside it, and finally to villas with swimming pools close to the village square when I decided that hanging about on beaches all day was just too uncomfortable at my age.

But in 1992, the year of the Barcelona Olympics, and before we had graduated to the comparative luxury of a villa with a pool, we rented a place on a farm just outside the village. That year, Frank, an Australian sports journalist and friend of Ron Atkin, was staying between workaday stints in Barcelona at Ron's villa near our lodgings.

One evening, Frank, Diana and I were finishing dinner in the square when Emma came to drive us home. She had left the car in the main car park and the car-park owner, who had given her the ticket to park, came along just behind her. An interesting bloke: he had two brothers, one a noted Spanish philosopher, the other an MEP. He himself, though equally well educated and fluent in English, was presumably less ambitious than his brothers and had settled for running a small bar in a street off the square and owning the car park. When we left he followed us and was installed in his kiosk as Emma drove the car out.

'Where is your ticket?' the man asked. None of us

could find it. 'Look,' I said, 'we'll go home, find the ticket and I'll come in and pay you tomorrow.'

'No,' he said. 'If you do not have the ticket you must pay for a whole day.'

'Don't be daft,' I said. 'You gave my daughter the ticket less than an hour ago.'

He was having none of this, so I told Emma to drive on, saying I'd sort it out the next day. She did and after a bit we realized the car-park owner was following us on his little pop-pop motorbike. When we stopped to let Frank out the man drew up alongside us.

'What,' I said, 'is your problem?'

'You must pay,' he said.

'Come on, we've been through this – we'll find the ticket and I'll pay you tomorrow.'

He drew himself up to his full height, or as near to full height as you can get when sitting on the saddle of a little pop-pop motorbike. 'You will never park in my car park again!' he said. We all laughed, and he swept away, bristling with outrage.

A couple of days later, Frank, who in the interim had been reporting on the Games in Barcelona, returned to the village, bringing with him a former Australian Olympic boxer named Benny who was covering the boxing for either Australian TV or a newspaper. Benny, who had enjoyed what can only be described as a very good night in Barcelona, had been poured into the car by Frank and woke the next morning not, as he had expected, in the middle of a bustling city but staring out at fields and sheep.

'Where the fuck am I?' he asked. Frank explained and said he would drive him to the village for breakfast. Which he did and, naturally, went to leave his car in the car park, only to find the car-park owner, recognizing him as one of the passengers in the Norman car, leaping out of his kiosk, pointing at him dramatically and shouting: 'You cannot come in here – you are banned!'

Benny was deeply impressed. 'Jesus, Frank,' he said, 'what the hell have you been up to? You've only been here five minutes and already you're banned from the fucking car park!'

We Normans, of course, have been banned from the fucking car park ever since, even though I did pay for the ticket.

Both girls have had an eclectic variety of jobs; Mamf began in publishing then moved into freelance journalism and television. She has written articles for *The Times*, the *Guardian*, the *Daily Mail*, the *Daily* and *Sunday Express* and for a while she and her sister were joint film critics for the *Daily Mirror*. For ITV, Mamfie and Anastasia Cooke co-presented *Dial Midnight*, an often rowdy chat show which, probably because of its two attractive blonde presenters, had an enthusiastic gay following. She has also been arts correspondent for *London Tonight* (again on ITV), a presenter on VH1 and was arts correspondent on a weekly show for Anglia Television.

I should point out here that neither in Mamf's case nor Emma's did nepotism play any part. If I could, I would certainly have used such fame as I had to get them jobs but, alas, I never had that much influence. The best I could do was arrange interviews for them with TV bosses, but all they led to was useful advice, never work. Whatever jobs the girls had, they got for themselves.

After university, Emma worked for a while at the film and TV company the Comic Strip as personal assistant to Peter Richardson, the versatile head honcho there. Then she decided that she, too, would like to be a journalist, so, without any experience, she applied for and got a job as staff writer on a magazine called *Your Amstrad PCW*. She ended up as its editor, then went on to edit a sister magazine *Video Today*. When she tired of that she went freelance, shared the *Daily Mirror* job with her sister, and later reviewed films and/or videos for Greater London Radio, a Radio 5 programme hosted by Johnny Walker, Sheridan Morley's Radio 2 show and Sky News. In the meantime she wrote a weekly video-review column for the *Radio Times* and co-authored a guide to films on TV with me.

But whatever they were doing, however busy they were, both girls still came with us on holiday to Sant

Martí and when the grandsons came along they grew to love the place, too.

One day we were all walking to the village square for lunch, Charlie, then aged six, and me tagging along at the rear, when he started talking about bullfighting.

'What I wish,' he said, 'is that the bullfighters would get killed and not the bull.'

'I see where you're coming from, Charlie,' I said, 'but, you know, bullfighters are very brave. Do you think you could be that brave?'

'No,' he said.

'I don't think I could either,' I said.

To which he replied: 'Well, you don't want to be a bullfighter – not at your age.' Immediately, any ambition I might have had to enrol at a night school for bullfighters was killed stone dead – and by an ageist six-year-old.

A few years later Harry and Charlie inveigled Diana and me into taking them on at tennis. Neither of us had played for years but we were giving them a sound beating when a ball came back over the net, both Diana and I yelled 'Mine!', both rushed at it, both missed it; I landed on her foot and fell heavily. When we had limped painfully off the court, she with a broken metatarsal, I with a cracked rib, she said coldly: 'That was *my* ball.'

'No, it wasn't,' I said. 'It was mine.' So it was – it was on my forehand, which was stronger than her backhand.

'It was *mine*,' she repeated firmly, and turned to the boys: 'Wasn't it?' And they, ever loath to gainsay their granny, said, 'Yes,' craven little buggers. So there again, as in everything where Diana and I disagreed, it turned out to be my fault. Just as well, I suppose, that I found her adamant refusal to accept that she could be wrong – ever – at first exasperating but ultimately always amusing.

It was Diana's habit on these holidays to take with her a large box filled with all manner of medicaments: bandages, plasters, ointments, creams, salves, constipation and/or diarrhoea cures, cough medicines, anti-mosquito sprays and, very possibly, splints. It was generally believed within the family that she carried enough stuff with her to perform a heart transplant if that should prove necessary. Unfortunately, even with all this equipment, there was very little she could do after the tennis match except slap soothing ointments and plasters on our scraped and bleeding arms and legs.

Her motto – probably the result of her time with the Girl Guides – was always to be prepared. Thus whenever there was even the remote prospect of snow she would load the boot of the car with shovels and blankets in case we got snowed in. If snow had actually fallen she would add a variety of drinks and a packet of Marmite sandwiches, even if we were only going to Stevenage to shop. 'You never know,' she would say ominously as we set off. She used to buy a lot of stuff from the Kleeneze man, landing us with a load of things for which we could never find a use. But even the Kleeneze man, grateful though he was for her custom, had to draw the line when one winter, with no snow even forecast, she saw in his catalogue some kind of one-piece, silver-coloured, thermally heated suit recommended presumably for those going to the Arctic. She immediately said she'd have one.

He refused to sell it to her. 'No, Mrs Norman,' he said firmly, regardless of his commission. 'Trust me, you really don't need one of those.'

Mind you, she wasn't that great as a Girl Guide. One year when she was aged twelve or thereabouts, she, as leader, lost an entire troop of Guides in the fog on Dartmoor.

Diana, ever enterprising, found her own way home all right. 'But what about the others?' I asked her. 'I really can't remember,' she said. No doubt they, too, got home safely, but the intriguing possibility remains that even today there might be a troop of now aged and probably savage Girl Guides roaming Dartmoor, terrorizing the tourists and living on roots and grubs.

15

Not Out

WHEN SHE WAS FIFTY, Diana, along with Sue Freathy and a few others, bought a 28-foot yacht called the *Jossalwasp* (whatever a Jossalwasp might be). Having been brought up by the sea in Devon with brothers who were both Sea Cadets, she had always been interested in sailing, an interest I did not remotely share. To me, sailing is best done (if at all) on an ocean-going liner with stewards bringing a constant supply of gin and tonic. So I never went with her on her yacht, though I did go and admire it at its berth in East Anglia. I don't think they took it to sea much, mostly cruising down the river Orwell and along the Thames.

These were happy times for Diana, because she took sailing seriously. She earned her Day Skipper's accreditation on a cross-Channel trip in a Force 8 gale when the rest of the crew were seasick and she was at the wheel for ten hours, battling the elements.

'That must have been bloody terrifying,' I said.

'No,' she said. 'I loved every minute of it.' Never mind bullfighting, I wouldn't have been brave enough to do what she did that day and night, crossing a distinctly cheesed-off Channel.

But just as I didn't share her free-time interests, she didn't share mine. Cricket was and always has been my thing. I played for Datchworth for twenty-five years, usually on ferocious, unprepared wickets. Once, opening the innings, I carried my bat for 12 out of a team total of 26. Another time, bowling leg-breaks, I did the hat trick – one caught, two stumped. Later, switching to off breaks, because leg spinners are generally too expensive to get much of a bowl in village cricket, I took a few five-fors (or, as the cineliterate among us like to call them, Michelles).

Diana had no interest in cricket, except occasionally when England were playing. She never came to Lord's with me and rarely watched me play for Datchworth, although one year she was persuaded to take on the job of match secretary for the village team. This ended in ignominy when one Saturday two teams turned up to play us at home. The decent solution would have been for us, the Datchworthies, to let the other two sides play each other while we did other stuff, like shopping with our wives. But, no, sod it, we thought, we want a game of cricket. So we arbitrarily chose one side to take on and the other shoved off in an understandable huff and never played us again. Diana resigned that evening.

Cricket took on a new dimension for me when, thanks to Eric Morecambe, I was invited to join the Lord's Taverners, which is perhaps the leading cricketing charity in the country, raising large amounts of money to help young disabled or disadvantaged people, distributing sports equipment, sporting wheelchairs and minibuses, and generally trying to provide what we call 'a sporting chance'. For me the incentive was that the Taverners elevens consisted largely of people who used to play for England, the kind of people who wouldn't normally be expected to welcome me into the same ground as themselves, let alone the same team.

But, in fact, my first experience of, as it were, pro-am cricket came before I joined the Taverners. I had been invited by Roy Castle to play for a showbiz/media team against the full Hampshire County Cricket side in a benefit match for its captain, Richard Gilliatt. The game was to take place on a Sunday afternoon at what was then Hampshire's county ground in Southampton. Me? Playing on a first-class ground? How could I refuse?

Hampshire batted first and I started pretty well, taking a running, diving catch to dismiss the beneficiary himself, a catch on which I was congratulated by his team mates at teatime. Hey, come on – when you're as indifferent a cricketer as I was, these brief moments of glory are to be treasured.

After a while Trevor Jesty, an excellent all-rounder who had played one-day internationals for England, came to the wicket and Roy tossed me the ball. 'Fancy a bowl?' Never had I even dreamed of bowling to an international batsman so, naturally, I said yes. And I have to say that I had him completely baffled: not one of my first three cunningly flighted, sharply spinning off breaks went for more than four runs (actually, I think, they each went for four runs). But, at the fourth, Jesty stepped down the wicket and hit it, high in the air, towards long-on where I had a fielder placed for just such an eventuality – a disc jockey, he was, from Radio Victory in Portsmouth.

He did practically everything right, this disc jockey – shuffled into position, kept his eye on the ball. The only thing a purist might have objected to was that, as the ball fell towards him he forgot to bring his hands together, so it went straight between them and hit him resoundingly in the middle of the forehead, whereupon he fell to the ground as if he'd been shot.

There was a moment of shocked silence in the pretty considerable crowd, and then Red Cross and St John's Ambulance workers came rushing out of the woodwork to tend to him, and we, his team mates, joined them to see if we could help. The only person who didn't run to the long-on boundary was Jesty, who remained at the wicket, impatiently tapping his bat against his pads. But after a while even he strolled over to join us and took me to one side.

'Did that ball go for four or six?' he asked.

I looked down at the stricken disc jockey whose eye-balls were spinning like Shane Warne's googly. 'How can you ask a question like that at a time like this?' I said. 'Look at this man – his brains are coming out of his ears!'

Jesty shot him a casual glance. 'Oh, he'll be all right,' he said. 'Now, did it go for four or six?'

'Actually,' I said, 'it went for four.'

'Oh, fuck it,' he said, and went back to the middle, leaving me to wonder what kind of hard men these professional cricketers could be if two runs in someone else's benefit match meant so much to them.

I soon learned. Not long after I joined the Taverners I was playing for them at a game in Kent when one of our batsmen, John (J.T.) Murray, the former England and Middlesex wicketkeeper, was hit on the foot by a ball from a pretty quick Kentish fast bowler. He hobbled from the field and was taken to hospital. Not long afterwards word came through that his foot was broken. I passed on this sad news to John Price, former England fast bowler and team mate of Murray at Middlesex. 'Typical of J.T.,' he said. 'He was all right against the short stuff but he never could play the yorker.' And that was all the sympathy the poor man got.

Cricketers, above all other sportsmen, tend to be

philosophical: the unpredictable nature of the game they play makes them so. You can be sitting in the changing room waiting to bat, knowing that the bowlers out there aren't half as good as the lot from whom you took a half-century in the last match, and then it's your turn at the wicket: you look confidently at the field deciding where to hit your first four and then you're out first ball to an absolute jaffa, the only one bowled by the opposing team all afternoon, and you trudge back to the pavilion, wondering, Where the hell did that come from?

It happens whatever level of cricket you play, and bowlers are just as vulnerable; they can be unplayable in one match and then, while bowling quite as well as before, be hammered all over the ground in the next. It just happens, and if you can't cope with that, then cricket is not for you.

I've played, without much distinction, with or against some of the great names in the game – Ian Botham, Dennis Lillee, Viv Richards, Derek Underwood, Colin Cowdrey, Bill and John Edrich, John Snow, Steve Waugh, Mike Gatting . . . the list goes on – and without exception they have all been remarkably decent to me, greeting my tiny triumphs (a wicket taken or a well-struck four) as if I had done this at Lord's in an Ashes match. The only proviso was that whatever I did they had to feel I was doing my best. Anything less and their warmth would have turned to contempt because, to them, quite properly, cricket is too important to be messed about with even in a charity match.

In my time with the Taverners (I gave up playing and took up umpiring instead when I was sixty) I had one memorable week: on the Sunday at Arundel, one of the prettiest cricket grounds in the world, I had Colin Cowdrey caught at mid-off for about 13. If he had scored 53 I'd have known he had gifted me his wicket, but even in a charity match Colin would never deliberately get himself out for 13 or so. No, he'd been totally bamboozled by my devilish flight and spin. Or so I like to think.

Then on the following Saturday at Scarborough I caught and bowled Mike Denness for six. Well, okay, if I hadn't caught that ball I would probably have ended up with a navel the size of a melon, because it came straight back at my midriff off the middle of Mike's bat at the speed of light. I only put my hands down there in self-protection, but the ball stuck. Two England captains in one week – not bad for a village off-spinner.

What made the occasion even greater was that my skipper that day was Brian Close, former captain of Yorkshire and England, and probably the hardest, toughest man who ever played cricket. On one famous occasion when he was fielding at short leg very close to the bat, the batsman took an almighty swipe and the ball hit Close smack on the head. But even as he fell to the ground he was yelling, 'Catch it!' to his team mates.

On this day, however, he came up to me, saying: 'Well caught! Ah wouldn't ha' put my hands behind a ball like that on a cold day like this.' That, I reckon, is the finest compliment any man has ever paid to another.

In all my years playing cricket I only came across two men I actively disliked, and that was in a game for Datchworth. I came in second wicket down and joined our opener and headmaster of the village school, Bob King, who modelled his game on that of Geoffrey Boycott, which is to say that when in doubt play forward defensively, or do that anyway, whether you're in doubt or not. I was in good form that day and had scored 46 when Bob nudged a two and finally reached the first half-century he had ever scored in any form of cricket. I completed the second run, ran round the bowler's wicket and was setting off down the pitch to congratulate Bob when the bowler picked up the ball, whipped off the bails and said: 'How's that, Dad?' And his father, the umpire, said: 'That's out, son.'

It was the sneakiest bit of gamesmanship I have ever come across, because I was clearly not attempting another run. But I'm happy to say I never came across either of those bastards again.

One final reflection on cricket: Harold Pinter, a devoted player and chairman of the Gaieties Club, whose team is composed of stage actors and writers, once said that for him it was better than sex. I can understand what he meant without altogether going along with him, because I don't quite see the analogy. Both are pastimes to be indulged in passionately but, when you get right down to it, the only other thing sex and cricket really have in common is the simple question of whether you're in – or out.

16

Canvassing with Jesus

WHEN DIANA AND I first moved to Datchworth you could have held a mass meeting of the local Labour Party in the telephone box outside the post office. But then enthusiastic kindred spirits such as the primary school headmaster, Bob King, and his wife, Thora, moved into the village and soon the numbers swelled to about a hundred.

Until 1979, our MP was Shirley (now Baroness) Williams and we invited her to a cheese and wine party (well, it was the seventies) and both Diana and I liked her immediately. Just before she left I asked her a question, to which she replied: 'I really don't know the answer to that but I'll find out for you.' She was the first MP I had ever met who admitted to being stuck for an answer, and I was impressed. But I also thought cynically, Yeah, right – you're the Secretary of State for

Education; you've got sod all else to do but find an answer to my question.

A few months later we invited her to another cheese and wine party and when she arrived she came straight up to me and said: 'You remember that question you asked me?' As it happened, I had totally forgotten what it was, but I thought it best to nod in agreement, and she said: 'Well, the answer is this . . .' and proceeded to give it. From then on Shirley was our favourite politician and has remained so ever since.

Mind you, belonging to the Labour Party wasn't always comfortable. At meetings Diana was often sneered at because of her articulacy and cut-glass accent, and at one meeting in our house she happened to see some intense little squirrel writing derogatory notes about how middle-class our home was. Presumably, we'd have been more acceptable if we'd been unable to compose complete sentences, dropped our aitches and used glottal stops and lived in a council house.

Unfortunately, that's the way the Labour Party was, particularly after the 1979 election – driven by left-wing extremists, who believed the working man was the salt of the earth and everyone else was to be viewed with contempt.

So when, in 1981, Shirley felt she had had enough of this and left Labour to join Roy Jenkins, David Owen and Bill Rodgers in forming the Social Democratic

Party, Diana and I followed, with consequences we could never have predicted.

Apparently, a convenor was urgently needed in Hertfordshire and at party headquarters Shirley was asked if there was anyone she could recommend. 'Oh, Diana Norman will do that,' she said airily.

Diana Norman had not been consulted; Diana Norman, in fact, had not the slightest idea what a convenor was or what he/she was supposed to do. But suddenly, her bleating protests swept aside, she found herself appointed. Inevitably, she did a splendid job, organizing events, holding meetings (often in our house), keeping in touch with sympathizers around the county, liaising with Lord David Cobbold of the local Liberal Party, and arranging with him a huge fundraiser in aid of both the Liberals and the Social Democrats in the grounds of David's stately home, Knebworth House.

I did my bit, too. In various general elections or by-elections I stomped around Stevenage spreading the message alongside my friend Robert Powell (he who played Jesus of Nazareth on TV), accompanied Roy Jenkins on a walkabout when he attempted to win Warrington in 1981 and spoke at a rally in Crosby when Shirley became the first Social Democrat to win a seat in Parliament in the 1981 by-election.

Diana, though, used me in a much more modest capacity as a chauffeur to pick up potential sympathetic voters from all over the place and take them to the polling booths, especially during the general election of 1983. Social Democrat HQ might have thought I was quite an important supporter, but Diana knew what I was really fit for.

We stayed with the party until near the end of the decade, when the two Davids – Steel, leading the Liberals, and Owen, leading the Social Democrats – both of whom we knew and liked, fell out, stood back and carefully shot each other in the foot. The result was virtually the end of the Social Democrats and the creation of a new party, the Liberal Democrats. For a year or two Diana and I were too disenchanted to care about any political outfit but eventually we joined the Lib-Dems, since when I have spoken at rallies for both Lord Paddy Ashdown and Charles Kennedy, when each was leader of the party. For her part, Diana, once she ceased to be the convenor for Hertfordshire, took no further active role in politics. We both saw ourselves as democrats rather than Liberals (with a capital L); neither of us could imagine voting Conservative and though, like much of the country, we welcomed the advent of New Labour in 1997, we were utterly dis-illusioned with Tony Blair when he took us into the unnecessary and very possibly illegal war with Iraq in 2003.

We joined the famous anti-war march in London that year, striding down the middle of Piccadilly behind the Boilermakers' Union (simply because they happened to be there in front of us) and much admiring the woman, a Joyce Grenfell fan, carrying the banner that said: 'George, don't do that.' We knew, as everyone but Blair and the egregious George Dubya Bush seemed to, that there was no evidence at all that Iraq had weapons of mass destruction, and we were not taken in when, no such weapons having been found, the deadly duo came up with an entirely new reason for the invasion of Iraq, claiming they did it to 'get rid of the tyrant Saddam'. Bullshit. Of course Saddam was a tyrant, but getting shot of him was not the reason for the invasion and, anyway, deposing him has hardly brought peace to the country and its people. If Blair wants to know his political legacy, it's that shameful war and the chaos it caused in the Middle East.

Meanwhile, despite the demands at various times of the Social Democrats and the magistracy and at all times of running the home and the family, Diana continued writing. Between 1980 and 1998 she produced eight novels under her married name and even managed to fit in a biography of Constance Markievicz with the title, borrowed from W. B. Yeats, *Terrible Beauty*. Markievicz, née Gore-Booth, was the wife of a Polish count and a member of the Irish Ascendancy, which is to say the privileged and the landowners, but very different from the others. She was a suffragette, a socialist and an Irish revolutionary nationalist, who threw in her lot with Sinn Féin, took part in the Easter Rising in Dublin in 1916, and in 1918 was the first woman elected to the British Parliament, although, being a member of Sinn Féin, she refused to take her seat. Later she became one of the first women in the world to hold a Cabinet position, as Minister of Labour of the Irish Republic, from 1919 to 1922.

When the book was published it was launched in Dublin with a reception at the Mansion House, hosted by the then Minister for Labour and future Taoiseach, Bertie Ahern. Later, again at the Mansion House, at a gathering to celebrate the seventy-fifth anniversary of the Easter Rising, Diana was the only Englishwoman among a group of Irish writers to be invited to talk about the role of women in Irish politics.

Diana first became interested in Markievicz when writing a series of articles for a magazine about women overlooked by history, of whom she insisted there were far too many. As an example of how meticulous she was, the book wasn't finished and published until 1987, although she began researching it in the early part of the decade.

I had been invited to Dublin to appear on *The Late Late Show*, hosted by Gay Byrne, probably the only television programme in the world that could boast practically a 100 per cent viewing figure. Between the original broadcast and the repeat a few days later it was reckoned that virtually everyone in Ireland watched it every week. Admittedly, the population at the time was only about 3 million, but even so.

In the Green Room while I was waiting to go on we met Christine Sheridan, who was then managing a pop group. Christine, daughter of a prominent journalist on the *Irish Times*, knows just about everybody in the arts, literary, film and media worlds in Dublin, and when Diana mentioned that she was thinking of writing a book about Markievicz, she remarked casually that she was friendly with numerous people who had actually known her and offered to introduce Diana to them. That's just the way it is in Dublin: everyone seems to know everyone else.

This led to Diana making several visits to Ireland, driving herself around the country, interviewing a large number of people and meeting, among many others, the playwright Frank McGuinness who, like Christine, became a family friend. For a time, he and Diana planned to write a one-woman show about Markievicz, based on Diana's book, to feature the actress Fiona Shaw. Unfortunately, Shaw said she wouldn't be available because of other commitments at the time they had in mind and so the project was dropped. I'm not sure Frank has ever totally forgiven her.

But a good few years later at an auction he came across a sketch either by or of Markievicz, done when she was serving one of her eleven prison sentences courtesy of His Majesty King George V, bought it and sent it to Diana, who gave it pride of place in our sitting room.

She and I were both enamoured of Ireland and its people. Never mind all the stupid jokes about thick Paddies, the Irish are the most articulate people I know and on the whole have a greater command of English than the English do. I once asked Frank Delaney why this was so, and he said: 'You must remember that when the English ruled Ireland we weren't allowed to speak our own language, we had to speak yours. So we decided to speak it a damn sight better than you do.' And that's what so many of them have done ever since. What's more, the Irish seem to have a belief, quite unknown to the English, that life is to be enjoyed and that formalities are best dispensed with.

For instance, on that first visit Diana and I made to Dublin, we were having lunch in the Shelborne Hotel when a small man, not much bigger than a leprechaun, wearing a dark green uniform, came to our table and introduced himself.

'Ah, Mr Norman,' he said. 'Good to meet you. My name's Christie, I'm the hall porter here. What are you doing at four o'clock this afternoon?'

I said, bewildered: 'Well, I don't know, Christie. I hadn't really made . . .'

'That's grand,' he said. 'I'll pick you up at four o'clock

and take you to meet my friend Mort, who runs the smallest pub in Dublin.'

As he went away, I thought, This would never happen at Claridge's, and then I thought, But it ought to happen at Claridge's, because there was something quite charming about the approach and Christie's confidence that I would go along with his plans. Which is what I did. Christie took us to Mort's pub, the Dawson Arms, which is not much bigger than a large sitting room and was then and probably still is now, though Mort is long gone, a wonderfully relaxed and welcoming place.

It has always been a source of pride to me that I have – or, anyway, had – a large following in Dublin. When I was working for the BBC, Diana and I went there often and I was frequently accosted in the street. When that happened in England people tended to rush up to me, blushing with embarrassment, and say: 'I just wanted to tell you, I'm a great fan of yours.' Sometimes they'd get confused and say: 'I just wanted to tell you, you're a great fan of mine,' but I knew what they meant.

In Dublin it was different. Someone would step up to me and say: 'Ah, Mr Norman, I watch your programme. Very nice. But there are just one or two things I'd like to take up with you . . .' And fifteen minutes later we'd still be there, arguing back and forth.

Particularly pleasing to me was that, generally speaking, what the Irish seemed to like about my show was not necessarily what I said but the way I said it. In other words, they approved of my use of English and, coming from them, that was a compliment to be cherished.

As an illustration of Irish literacy, I offer you this, a perfectly true story. In Camden Town, North London, there was (maybe still is) a cinema that specialized in art-house movies, a bold thing to do because, to put it mildly, this is not a particularly affluent or educated middle-class area. Around the cinema and the nearby Tube station there was a large number of tramps and otherwise homeless men, the most feared among them being a big, drunken Irishman, an unfriendly fellow, all flowing, matted black hair and beard, and dark, filthy clothing.

One day when it was raining very hard he wandered into the cinema and started looking at the posters on the foyer walls. The two young women in the box office were terrified and phoned the manager in his office upstairs. 'Come down quick,' they said, 'the Irishman's in the foyer!'

The manager came down and approached the intruder. 'Can I help you, sir?'

The Irishman stroked his beard. 'Ah, sure,' he said, 'I was thinking I might come in and watch the fillum.'

'Well, of course, you're very welcome,' said the manager, 'but perhaps I should warn you – it might not be your cup of tea. You see, it's a European documentary with subtitles about a Dutch painter called Bruegel.'

The Irishman nodded. 'Ah, Bruegel, is it? Sure, you're right – not my cup of tea at all.' Then a pause and . . . 'Had it been Modigliani, however . . .' And he walked out. I defy you to find me an English tramp who could have come up with such a devastating and grammatically correct response.

17

Ariana Franklin

Iᴛ ᴡᴀs ɪɴ the new millennium that Diana finally got the recognition she deserved, but she had to change her name to do it.

She had continued writing her historical novels (eleven in all) until 2006, but she had always wanted to write thrillers, mystery stories, and her chance to do so came unexpectedly. Helen Heller, a British literary agent residing in Toronto, contacted Diana's then publisher, Susan Watt, at HarperCollins, asking if she could recommend a writer – a really good writer – who might be interested in weaving a thriller around the Grand Duchess Anastasia and what happened to her after the Russian Revolution. Susan recommended Diana, and she, when approached, was enthusiastic, not necessarily about Helen's original idea but about the general concept. Anastasia, daughter of the last Czar of

Russia, was thought by many to have escaped the general massacre of her family in 1917 but had never been heard of again. In *City of Shadows* Diana set her murder mystery story in Berlin in 1923, introduced an enigmatic Anastasia and threw in some smart twists and turns before wrapping it all up most satisfactorily. The novel, which came out in 2006 and was dedicated to Frank McGuinness, has never been published in this country but went down well in America and Canada.

The problem with this book, however, was that it was completely different from anything she had written before. If it had appeared under the name of Diana Norman it might well have disappointed her devoted followers, who would have been expecting something set further back in time. So a change of name was decided upon; *City of Shadows* was to appear as if written by an entirely new author.

But what should this author be called? Diana could have chosen Diana Narracott but wanted instead to use her mother's maiden name, Aeron Franklin. Helen approved of Franklin, arguing that it came earlier in the alphabet than either Narracott or Norman and the books would therefore be on a higher shelf in the shops, thus precluding the necessity for potential buyers to bend down and look for them. But Aeron (pronounced Eye-ron), she thought, might be too difficult for people to get their tongues around so, after some discussion, Ariana was chosen as a compromise.

Thus Ariana Franklin was born, but where was she to go from here? Diana was not much interested in writing further about the twentieth century, and neither was Ariana. What fascinated Diana, of course, were the twelfth century and Henry II and, by a remarkable coincidence, they fascinated Ariana, too. So it was back to the drawing board, back to research and the London Library to read even more voraciously about the twelfth century, until she came upon the Schola Medica Salernitana, a medical school in the Italian town of Salerno founded in the ninth century. Blissfully (for Ariana), even back then it took female students, along with Jews, Muslims, Christians – you name it – mixing Greco-Roman medical knowledge with Arab and Jewish traditions. A woman doctor – no, more than that, a female pathologist, no less – in twelfth-century England? Unheard of. But not in twelfth-century Salerno. And so Adelia Aguilar, Mistress of the Art of Death, sprang to life.

Mistress of the Art of Death. The title was Helen's idea and at first Diana disliked it. Too flamboyant, she thought. But readers on both sides of the Atlantic and beyond seized avidly upon it and the story, in which Adelia solves a number of mysterious murders in Cambridge, and so did the critics. The book found its way into the *New York Times* bestseller list and in the *NYT* itself the writer Sharon Kay Penman described it as 'one of the most compelling, suspenseful mysteries

I've read in years. Adelia is a wonderful character and I cannot wait for her next adventure.' In the same paper Kate Mosse said it 'succeeds in vividly bringing the twelfth century to life'. Another writer, Karen Harper, called it 'the mediaeval answer to Kay Scarpetta and the CSI detectives'. For *USA Today*, it was simply 'fascinating ... a rollicking microcosm of budding science, mediaeval culture and edge-of-your-seat suspense'. And so on.

The book was published in 2007 and Diana/Ariana was nominated in Britain by the Crime Writers' Association for the Ellis Peters Award for the best historical thriller that year. She knew, of course, that she couldn't possibly win but accepted the nomination as honour enough and decided to enjoy the party at which the winner would be announced.

I went with her, and it was a good party, plenty of food and drink. Indeed, Diana was leaning happily against the wall with two or three glasses of champagne inside her and not taking much notice at all when the announcement came: 'And the winner is ... Ariana Franklin!'

She was genuinely astonished but managed to find her way to the microphone and deliver a sober and impromptu – because she had prepared nothing – speech of thanks. It was one of the proudest moments of my life and when a few minutes later one of the judges, Sir Bernard Ingham, formerly Margaret

Above: Messing around in the hammock with Bertie.

Below: Dee and the grandchildren fishing for crabs in Padstow.

This was Diana's favourite photo of me – it hung in her office.

Above: Aboard a cruise with Christopher Lee and Shirley Ann Field (centre).

Below: Receiving my honorary doctorate from the University of East Anglia, with Emma on the left and Mamf on the right – another of Dee's favourite photos.

On the Orient Express. As you can see, books were very much in evidence on this excursion; Diana was an avid reader, as am I.

I'm not sure what the joke was, but we were clearly all enjoying it! In our lounge in Datchworth.

Above: In Bruges, with Christine.

Below: In her element. Diana loved sailing and she and a group of friends even bought their own yacht.

Above: The wedding of Diana's niece, Catherine. Dee clearly loved walking through the sabre arch.

Left: Me, Emma and Bertie in New York. He didn't wanna walk!

Below: Mamf and Emma.

My wife and the best friend a man could ever hope for.

Thatcher's press secretary, came past me, I thanked him. He just shrugged. 'It was no contest,' he said, and walked on.

Now Diana's life – or, anyway, her status – changed. She had always been highly regarded, well respected, but hitherto even when people were writing nice things about her work she had mostly been described as 'Barry Norman's wife', I being better-known than she was. This had always been nonsense. It irritated me, even if it didn't noticeably irritate her, because what she achieved had nothing to do with me. She was never riding on the coat-tails of what fame I enjoyed: she had done it all by herself.

But now, with the success of *Mistress of the Art of Death*, which also won awards in Sweden and the USA, and the three succeeding Aguilar novels, *The Death Maze*, *Relics of the Dead* and *A Murderous Procession*, she was hugely in demand at literary festivals and the like, and this astonished her, too. 'I'm not used to being feted,' she said. 'Being married to a TV presenter, I'm more accustomed to being trampled in the rush to get his autograph than being publicized myself.' A slight pause here, and then . . . 'I'm not complaining, though.'

Neither was I. In the summer before she was taken seriously ill I went with her to the Crime Writing Festival in Harrogate and, apart from the fact that I chaired one discussion there, nobody paid me the slightest attention. They were only interested in Diana and I was just the bloke she'd brought along with her. I couldn't have been more pleased.

Of her books, she once said: 'The lovely thing about the twelfth century is that you don't have to go too far to find wonderful plots. I always plot first. If you're writing thrillers, which, of all the genres, have to be well constructed, and not streams of consciousness, you've got to know where you're going. I have the last line of the book in my head before I sit down to write, and I stagger towards it like a drunk navigating furniture to get to the far side of the room.'

She never had any truck with the 'Gadzooks!' and 'Prithee, sire' school of historical novels, saying: 'The characters sounded contemporary to each other, so why shouldn't they sound contemporary to us? On the other hand, you mustn't use slang because that can jar the reader into the present day. It's tricky.'

Her method of writing was typically idiosyncratic. Whenever possible she would go into her study at about 9 a.m. and work until she felt she'd done enough for the day. This process always included going to bed for an hour or so after lunch, armed with notebook and pen, for what she described as 'plotting' time. Quite often I would look in on her to find her 'plotting' peacefully with her eyes closed, the notebook discarded and the pen leaking on to the duvet.

In fact, what she came to call 'plotting time' had started off as 'solidarity with the nurses'. Many, many years before, the nation's nurses, protesting quite rightly about appalling conditions and pay, had threatened to go on strike for an hour or two every afternoon. They never did, but Diana thought it was an excellent idea and forever after, out of solidarity, took to her bed for an hour or so every day, often complaining that the ungrateful nurses, who she thought had chickened out of striking, had no idea of the sacrifice she was making on their behalf.

In addition to the normal working day, she would frequently get up around 2 a.m. and work away for a couple of hours. There was never a fixed routine; the only thing the family could rely on was that every so often she would come stomping out of her study complaining either that a) any talent she'd ever possessed had mysteriously vanished or b) the world was conspiring to make it impossible for her to finish the book.

What the latter meant was that either her best friend Mary Poole, an American teacher who lived a few streets away, had invited her for tea, or that another friend had asked if she could just drop in for a minute. She was never known to say no to any of these requests, no matter how often I urged her to be more ruthless in future, to tell everyone that she was working and not just messing about on a word processor for fun. The friends, Mary in particular, would have understood, but Diana just couldn't do that. Nor could she resist breaking off her work to babysit for Harry and Charlie, pick up Bertie from school or send an immediate reply to her many electronic penfriends and admirers.

But out of this apparently chaotic method came a series of brilliant novels which ultimately brought her one of the Crime Writers' Association's most coveted prizes, the Dagger in the Library, awarded for the body of her work. Before that, however, as Ariana Franklin's popularity increased, her publishers sent her to Toronto for a series of meetings with booksellers and journalists and, prior to that, in 2007 to America on a similar, more breathless, expedition, which involved visiting about six cities in a week, beginning in Detroit, taking in the likes of Memphis and ending in Boston.

Diana didn't want to go on either of these alone, even though Helen was in constant attendance in Toronto, so she took me with her. She had never, in truth, been a great traveller and was always happiest at home in Datchworth. When I was working in television, for instance, she would never join me on my trips to Los Angeles, finding California of no interest to her whatsoever, and it had taken me years to persuade her to go to New York.

When, reluctantly, she at last agreed to join me there she turned up late one afternoon in my room at the Algonquin Hotel, slightly jet-lagged and complaining that she had no toothpaste.

'No problem,' I said, 'there's a drugstore just round the corner.' So we went to the drugstore and as we came out an unmarked police car came speeding along Sixth Avenue, siren screeching, passenger leaning out to attach the flashing light to the roof, and went racing up West 44th Street. Diana watched, mouth agape, deeply impressed. This was something straight out of *Kojak*.

When we got back to the hotel I pressed the button for the lift and we waited. You always had to wait for the lift at the Algonquin, because it took its time. The actor Charles Laughton once stayed there for a few years and said he spent half that time waiting for the elevator.

Anyway, Diana and I had been waiting for a few minutes when Tony, the hotel bell captain, drifted up. 'Anyone pressed for the elevator?' he asked. I said I had. 'Okay,' he said, 'I'll do it again.' Press, press. 'He hates that, the elevator man, when people keep pressing the button.' Press, press. 'It really makes him mad.' Press, press. Diana and I were watching in astonishment as he kept pressing the button. 'Tell you what,' Tony said, 'when he gets here, nobody knows who did it, right?' 'Right,' we said. A moment later the elevator arrived and the ancient liftman glowered out at us, whereupon Tony pointed at Diana and said: 'She did it, she did it!' Right then, Diana developed an instant love affair with the city.

She loved it even more a few days later when, leaving the Guggenheim Museum, we decided to take a bus back to downtown Manhattan. The fare was 90 cents and you were supposed to have either a token or the exact money. I had neither. The driver, a scowling young black man – well, of course he was scowling; he was a New Yorker – refused to take the two dollar bills I offered him. 'I can't give you change,' he said. 'Never mind,' I said. 'Keep it.'

'I wish I could, but I can't.' What to do then? 'Get on the bus and siddown,' he said.

About half a mile along the road he turned towards me. 'You still owe me.'

'I know. We've already established that,' I said. 'I haven't got the exact fare and you won't give me any change. So what are we going to do?'

He glared at me contemptuously. 'Ask the people on the bus,' he said. 'Use your initiative.' So I did. I held up my dollar bills and somehow, with coins being eagerly pressed upon me from all over the bus, ended up with a load of nickels, dimes and quarters.

By the time I'd given the driver his $1.80 I still had about 75 cents left over, to say nothing of two senior citizens' bus passes that had been generously thrust into my hand. Meanwhile, Diana had been armed with a handy phrase to use against me. From then on, whenever I hesitated over some decision, 'Use your initiative!' she'd say.

One year we were in the city with Emma and the then four-year-old Bertie and decided, it being a nice day, to have a stroll round Central Park. We pushed Bertie in his buggy up Fifth Avenue and, having arrived at the park, told him to get out and walk.

'I don't want to walk,' he said. 'Well, you've got to,' we told him. 'You need the exercise and, anyway, it's nice here, plenty of fresh air and trees and grass. Look, Bertie – squirrels, lots of squirrels.' He was not to be moved. 'I don't want to walk,' he said.

We gritted our teeth. 'Bertie,' we said, 'get out and walk.' And at that moment a huge wino – a bum, a hobo – reared up from a bench nearby and yelled: 'He don't wanna walk! Why you makin' him walk?'

'Bertie,' we hissed, grabbing him. 'Walk.'

'He don't wanna walk,' said the bum.

'Bertie,' we said, 'don't walk – run!'

'Why you makin' him walk?' cried the bum. Then he turned to his fellow bums on the bench. 'They makin' him walk and he don't wanna walk!' They all rose as one bum and we fled across the park, dragging Bertie by the hands, pursued by an irate chorus of: 'He don't wanna walk! Why you makin' him walk?'

Hey, but that's New York for you – and so was the reaction we got to the reins we put on Bertie. Emma had brought them because he was much given to wandering off on his own, regardless of what anyone else was doing. In this way we had, at home, temporarily lost him not only in supermarkets but in quite small shops, with resulting periods of panic, and we weren't about to let that happen in New York.

Once we'd escaped the bums we put the reins on him

in Central Park and a middle-class mother, with two small children about Bertie's age, gazed upon them with envy. 'Ah, gee, where'd you get those?' she asked. 'Where can I get those for my kids?' Reins, it seemed, were not to be bought in New York, and a possible explanation for this dawned upon us the same day when we took Bertie, reined, to Macy's department store, where a pretty young black shop assistant confronted us angrily.

'What are you doing?' she said. 'You're treating that child like a dog. You're robbing him of his freedom.' As Diana said, there didn't seem much point in explaining to her that at that age freedom for Bertie meant the liberty to slide away on to Broadway, probably never to be seen again by his family.

So, for a variety of reasons, Diana loved New York. She spent hours researching her novels in the public library at the top of 42nd Street, usually lunched off New England clam chowder in the Oyster Bar under Grand Central Station and took frequent trips – again for research reasons – to The Cloisters, the museum in Washington Heights that houses a magnificent collection of mediaeval art, manuscripts and books.

And because of her enthusiasm I grew to love the city too. Before her first visit I had been there several times, without developing any kind of affection for the place. But now, seeing it vicariously through her eyes, I warmed to its charms. It's brash, fast-moving, pulsating with energy, rude, in-yer-face, get-outta-my-face, funny, sophisticated and unlike anywhere else in America. For heaven's sake, they even understand irony there, which hardly any other place in the USA seems to do. It's unique and, thanks to a great extent to Diana's vision and understanding, whenever I was there without her and had a free day I would walk for hours along the streets and avenues, making frequent stops in bookshops, coffee shops and delis and constantly remembering to look up, because the view of Manhattan's skyscrapers when seen from street level is always breathtaking. Some of my New York friends describe it as 'the most western city in Europe' and the polyglot population lends some strength to such a view but, in fact, they're wrong. There's nothing like it in Europe. Only in America . . .

18

Accidents and Emergencies

FOR MANY YEARS Diana had suffered from a serious heart problem, a blocked branch bundle, which sounds vaguely comical but, believe me, is not. Its most obvious manifestation was fibrillation, twitching of the muscles in the heart, but generally speaking she was able to keep this under control with daily medication. She never complained about it and, in fact, only ever mentioned it when the fibrillation was particularly severe. On the whole she made very little of it and, therefore, to my shame, so did I. I was, I suppose, as Americans would put it, in denial.

The point is that Dee didn't take nearly enough care of herself and, consequently, neither did I of her, though I'm still not sure what I could have done. Certainly, I worried about her; indeed, worry and fear have been my constant companions through much of my life: not worry and fear for myself but for those near and dear to me – for my parents, brother and sister when I was young and then for Diana, the girls and the grandsons later on.

She first told me about her heart condition one evening in the early eighties at King's Cross Station as we waited for a train home. I had come from work, she from the hospital where she had been diagnosed.

'Hey, I must tell you what happened today,' I said, and babbled on, only pausing when I realized she wasn't finding whatever it was nearly as funny as I did. 'What's up?'

'I've got something wrong with my heart,' she said, and immediately I thought: Of course. She's been to the hospital. Why didn't I ask her about that right away? How could I have been so insensitive? What the hell's the matter with me?

We talked about it. She told me of the treatment involved and how she had to go back to hospital for further tests. I knew it was serious, very serious, but my mind veered away from the gravity of it all and seized instead on the comfort offered by her remark that, with proper care and attention, she could live with the condition for a good many years. Denial already, I suppose, though there couldn't have been too much denial, because I've remembered that moment, that conversation on number ten platform at King's Cross, ever since.

Thankfully, bouts of fibrillation apart, Diana's health

continued to be very good, although I often had to remind her that she was due for another consultation with her cardiologist. 'Oh, I haven't got time,' she would say impatiently, time and the lack of it being among her main preoccupations as her success as a novelist grew and the publishers wanted more books.

'Well, make the bloody time,' I would say, and then we would squabble irritably for a few days until finally she gave in.

But during the first decade of the new millennium she was twice admitted to hospital, first with pneumonia, then a few weeks later when she looked so unwell that I drove her to A&E, where it was discovered that the oxygen level in her blood was down to 50 per cent.

For the first few days on that second occasion they put her in the geriatric ward, presumably because of her age and the lack of beds anywhere else. Even though until the day she died she never remotely looked or sounded like a geriatric, she didn't mind too much, except when someone – probably not one of the geriatrics but a hospital worker – stole her slippers, souvenirs of a trip to New York on the QE2, and she did rather object to the fact that one old woman kept shouting all the time while another, a couple of beds down, was farting noxiously day and night. Otherwise, she made no fuss but then she rarely did except when a bank or a trading or utilities company upset her, and then she would write them what she called 'one of my letters'. These, I am here to tell you, were not letters you would want to receive, written in cold fury and brooking no argument.

When she left hospital the second time, her cardiologist, Mary Lynch, gave her a stern talking-to, telling her that her heart was getting weaker and that she should take things much more easily in future. Diana listened meekly, promised to follow her advice and then, once home, promptly ignored it. Taking things easy was never her way. Had she done so she might have lived a fair bit longer but, then again, maybe not. When she set her mind on something it had to be done – like *now*. Having to abandon whatever project she'd decided upon because it might tire her would have left her so irritable that she could well have died of sheer frustration.

By the same token, if she wanted me to do something, it, too, had to be done now. 'Are you going to take the rubbish out?' she would ask. And I would say: 'Yeah, in a minute.'

Five minutes later . . . 'Well, when are you going to take the rubbish out?'

'Any second now, as soon as there's a commercial break in the cricket.'

Five minutes after that she's in the kitchen hoisting the sack of rubbish out of its bin and muttering: 'Oh, never mind, I'll do it myself. As usual.'

The 'as usual' was, of course, an exaggeration. What

'as usual' really meant was that I, chuntering and cursing and seeking a quiet life, would hoist myself out of my chair and take the bloody rubbish to its collection point at the end of the garden, and then discover when I got back indoors that Graeme Swann had taken two wickets in my absence and I'd even missed the replays.

Still, occasional bouts of fibrillation apart, she stayed pretty fit. Well, there was the time in 2009 when we'd been to our next-door neighbours, Giles and Carole Peacock, for supper and, on leaving in the dark, stupidly declined their offer of the loan of a torch, there being no street lights where we lived. 'Good Lord, no,' Diana said. 'We don't need a torch. It's only a few yards.' So it was, but in those few yards was a pothole, into which she tripped and fell.

'Serves you right,' I said, unsympathetically. 'We should have taken the torch.' Indeed we should, because her foot hurt when she put it to the ground, and the next day at the Lister Hospital's A&E in Stevenage it was discovered that she'd broken a metatarsal. She left the place on crutches and with her leg in plaster. Red plaster was the colour she'd chosen, saying, 'If you've got it, flaunt it.' For days she went about complaining bitterly about the crutches.

I thought I'd cheer her up by telling her that hers was exactly the same injury as David Beckham and Wayne Rooney had suffered, although theirs weren't contracted by tripping over potholes.

'Yes, that's all very well,' she said. 'But I bet bloody Wayne Rooney and Beckham had servants to look after them.'

Actually, she did have a servant – me. While she was incapacitated I did the shopping, the ferrying around and most of the cooking, but I don't think she counted that. What else was a husband for, after all?

In June that year we celebrated fifty years in Datchworth with a party in our garden. Diana's brother Roger and his wife, Anne, were among the guests that day, and their presence lent a sharp poignancy to what was otherwise a pretty cheerful occasion because we were all aware that this was almost certainly the last time Roger would ever come to our home.

Earlier in the year he had been diagnosed with mesothelioma, a form of cancer caused by exposure to asbestos, which he had contracted some thirty years earlier while serving in the Royal Navy. It can lie dormant for decades but once it's diagnosed the sufferer can usually expect no more than a year to live. Roger had been diagnosed a few months previously.

In late July, we – that is, Diana, the girls, the three boys, Woody and I – took our regular annual holiday in Sant Martí, renting the usual villa with pool on the outskirts of the village. As a holiday, it started badly and ended worse.

Normally, the others would fly to Gerona and there rent a couple of cars while Diana and I made a more leisurely way to Spain – Eurotunnel to Calais, lunch and a little shopping in Boulogne then back to Calais to catch the car train to Narbonne. Next morning we would arrive in warm sunshine, breakfast at the station buffet while the car was unloaded, then drive the hundred or so miles over the Pyrenees, pausing to stock up with supplies of food and drink and have lunch at the vast Auchan supermarket in Perpignan. A very civilized way to do it, we thought, but that year French Rail had cancelled the Narbonne car train so, for the first time, we all flew to Gerona together via Ryanair.

Initially, at least, we were among the lucky ones, in that we did get on the plane and it did take off. Later that day there was such chaos at Stansted Airport that hundreds of people – among them an irate David Dimbleby, presenter of BBC1's *Question Time* – missed their flights entirely.

The first bad news when we reached Gerona was that Ryanair had left Bertie's suitcase behind and, despite their protestations that it would be with us via the next flight, we didn't get it back for three days.

There was also the business of the damaged hire car, which I mentioned earlier. The reason Emma had to return it at the end of the holiday was that her mum and I were long gone by then. Diana had been unhappy from the start. Roger was in hospital in Portsmouth with God alone knew how long to live. She phoned him or Anne every day, consumed with guilt. 'I shouldn't have come on holiday,' she said. 'I should have stayed with him.'

We were booked into the villa for two weeks but before the end of the first she wanted to go home, so we did. It cost us, I may say, an arm and a leg. No refund on the return tickets we had already bought; we had to book again at the full price, then pay a surcharge for not having booked online. Panic as we checked in lest our luggage was half a kilo overweight and we'd either have to leave stuff behind or pay a ransom to get it on the plane. One way or another, they get you coming and going.

There is, I know, much to be said for Ryanair and its price structure, if you travel light. But, frankly, it's not the most user-friendly airline in the world and if you – well, not you but your luggage – is at all overweight, it'll cost you plenty. Come to that, I can easily foresee a day when Ryanair will start weighing the passengers, too, and, if they're over what the airline deems a reasonable weight, they'll have to pay a surcharge to get themselves on the plane.

Luckily, Diana and I were okay as far as luggage weight went, but I was in a disgruntled mood after a truncated, pretty miserable and anxious holiday, not to mention what is now the default attitude of airports all over the world – that passengers must be treated as recalcitrant cattle each with an IQ no greater than his or her shoe size.

I can remember when flying used to be fun, though maybe that was because in those days either the BBC or, later, Sky paid for the flight and I travelled business class or, with Virgin Airlines, upper class, and several times on Concorde. I was used to VIP treatment and as close to luxury as air travel can ever be. Now, using economy airlines, I suffered a culture shock. You queue to check in, queue to get through security and queue again probably for half an hour to get aboard the plane, after which it's every man for himself as you struggle to find two seats next to each other. And that's how it was at Gerona.

So when we touched down at Stansted and the air stewardess (or whatever they call themselves these days) thanked us all for 'choosing to fly Ryanair' I felt obliged to say: 'What do you mean – choosing? This is the only bloody airline that flies between Gerona and Stansted. We *had* no choice.'

The day after we returned home we drove to Portsmouth to see Roger. Anne, Tony and his wife Margaret were there, too. Roger was amazing: desperately ill, painfully thin but totally lacking in self-pity. While we were with him his doctor came in to tell him, in effect, that there was very little more they could do for him. The only question really was whether he wanted to stay in the hospital, be moved to a hospice or go home. Roger was adamant. 'I want to die at home,' he said.

So it was arranged and so, I believe, Diana's final, fatal problems began. Over the next several weeks, until his death in September, she drove down at least twice a week to Southampton to help Anne and his NHS carers tend to him. Once or twice she stayed overnight or even for a few days, but mostly she drove home again on the same day, a round trip of comfortably more than 200 miles, added to several hours of quite hard work and great anxiety. It was, pretty self-evidently, far too much for a woman of seventy-six with heart problems, but there was no dissuading her. She loved her brothers, had always been the big sister they looked up to, and she wasn't about to let Roger down now.

I don't think she was ever really well after his death. She wouldn't admit to it for several weeks, although in October she woke up one morning with pain in all her joints. It was diagnosed, wrongly, as osteoarthritis, came and went and eventually died away. What in fact it was, as we learned later, was an early sign of vasculitis, but the doctor who misdiagnosed her could hardly be blamed because, we were told, vasculitis is comparatively rare and few GPs know much, if anything, about it. Unfortunately, it also tends to be fatal.

And so the year wore on.

Christmas was a traditional, happy, family affair. New Year's Eve, as usual, we went to bed early. Neither of us could see the point of exuberant celebrations on New Year's Eve. I mean, for God's sake, when you wake up on 1 January it's not as if your worries, problems and debts of the previous year have been miraculously wiped out. You've still got them all and, on top of that, you've probably got a monumental hangover as well, plus the Christmas credit-card bills to pay, as well as, if you're self-employed, your income tax before the month is out. What's to celebrate?

Quite soon in the New Year, Diana's health began to decline. She complained of weariness and a permanent thirst. Armed with no medical knowledge whatsoever, I suggested this might be late-onset diabetes and urged her to arrange a blood test. She said she would. A few days later I asked her when the test was to be. 'I'm feeling a bit better,' she lied, 'but I'll fix it up next week.'

Next week, same thing. And the week after. Then one day she came to me and said, most uncharacteristically: 'I'm really not feeling at all well.' By now she had actually arranged a blood test, but not for several days. As it happened, I was to have the sort of test I'd been urging on her the following morning. In my case it was merely routine, something GPs recommend old crumblies to have every year. 'You take my test,' I said, 'and I'll take yours.'

She had the test the next morning. Normally, you don't get any feedback on these things for about a week, but this time the GP was on the phone to Diana early that afternoon. Exactly what the problem was Diana didn't tell me, but the doctor had told her to start taking certain antibiotics as a matter of urgency.

The following day, a Saturday, we were due to go to Birmingham for a fortieth wedding anniversary party for Roger and Sandra Partridge. Their son Adam had asked us to attend as surprise guests. 'We're not going,' I said. 'No chance. You're not well enough. I'll call Adam and explain.'

'No,' she said, 'we must go. Roger would never forgive me if we didn't.' We argued. She won, as she usually did. We went to Birmingham – Diana driving, of course – put up at a hotel, went to the party, had a nice time, and the next day she drove us home again.

Monday morning she got a phone call from the doctor's surgery in Knebworth. The full results of her blood test were in and she was to run, not walk, to the nearest A&E, because she was in imminent danger of kidney failure.

And from then on the year simply got worse.

What she had this first time around was renal vasculitis, vasculitis being a complaint that attacks the blood vessels, not just in the kidneys but anywhere, causing them to swell. She was in the Lister's renal unit for about a week, during which time I not only visited her every day but very nearly joined her.

One night during hospital visiting hours, Emma driving, we parked across the road from the A&E unit, which turned out to be handy really, because, crossing this wide, unlit road, I failed to see a bloody great intersection in the middle, tripped over it and landed partly on my nose and partly on my right side. A couple of passers-by dashed across to help Emma get me to my feet and, leaning heavily on her, I staggered into the A&E, blood pouring from my nose and a pain in my side which I just knew was a cracked rib, because I'd cracked a rib at least four times previously. Emma stayed with me while I checked in and was asked to wait, and then she dashed upstairs to the renal unit, there to be greeted by a much better – because she was soon to be released – but irate mother. It didn't help matters that Emma was giggling at the absurdity of the situation.

'Oh, thanks very much for coming,' Diana said with heavy sarcasm. 'Look at the time – visiting hours are over in five minutes. Can't think why you bothered. And where's your father? You might as well go home now.'

Em explained, and anger changed to worry. 'Get me a wheelchair,' Diana said. 'I must go and see him.'

And so we met in the corridor outside her ward, she in a wheelchair, me covered in dried blood. Well, I'd got fed up with waiting and, besides, there's damn all doctors can do about broken noses and cracked ribs, as I know, having suffered both enough times.

When Diana came home she seemed fine, although her renal consultant, Dr Paul Warwicker, had started her on what was scheduled to be a three-month course of steroids and aggressive chemotherapy, because, as she explained to a friend, 'my immune system has turned on me like the treacherous dog it is'. Also, because, her immune system being down, she was liable to contract any cold, cough or virus that was going around, she moaned: 'Barry's threatening not to let anybody into the house or allow me out of it.' In addition to that I had to take her to the hospital almost daily for check-ups. As it turned out, that was rather encouraging, because they were pretty happy with her, one doctor saying: 'Let's put it like this – I wouldn't be surprised if you were on dialysis next week, but I'd be very surprised if you were still on it next year.'

'Bloody dialysis,' Diana said as we left. 'That's all I need. When will I ever get any work done?' She rarely complained about her health but complained bitterly when that health stopped her doing what she wanted – writing, obviously, and attending literary festivals, for which she was by now in much demand.

In fact, the question of dialysis never really arose because she was only home for a week or so.

We slept separately, for no other reason than that she said my snoring kept her awake and, though I denied strenuously that I ever snored and even claimed that she was not entirely guiltless in this area herself, I had to concede eventually that perhaps I did snore occasionally. What forced this confession, I suppose, was her habit of rousing me from a deep sleep by punching me viciously in the ribs in the middle of the night, hissing: 'Turn over. You're snoring!'

So we slept apart and, on the morning of 7 April 2010, I was awoken by the phone ringing in my bedroom. It was Emma asking: 'What's wrong with Mum? She just called me and said she couldn't see to read.'

I got up at once and found Diana wandering along the landing, somehow looking simultaneously cross and dazed and complaining of a splitting headache, so bad that she couldn't focus to read. 'I think I'm having a migraine,' she said.

I knew that was improbable; she'd never suffered from migraine in her life. My fear was that she was having a stroke. I put her back into bed and tried to take her blood pressure with one of those home kits. Nothing registered.

By now Emma was on the phone again. 'Call an ambulance,' she said, and I, panicking, said: 'What do you dial – 911, isn't it?' (Christ, I watch far too many American movies.)

'I don't want a fucking ambulance!' Diana said as I dialled 999, and she was still saying it when the fucking ambulance arrived and the medic came into the bedroom to take her blood pressure with a proper, professional instrument. The result was terrifying – pretty nearly off the scale.

'Right,' said the medic. 'No way I'm leaving her here with blood pressure like that.'

He and the young female driver put her on a stretcher and carried her, still protesting bitterly that she'd be all right in a little while, to the ambulance, and I threw on some clothes and went with them.

I sat there in the back of the ambulance holding her hand while the medic tended to her, doing God knows what, I can't remember, and then – the most touching, terrifying moment on that dreadful drive – she gave me a sweet, imploring yet frightened smile, as if something was happening to her that she couldn't begin to comprehend, and began jerking spasmodically.

'She's fitting!' said the medic to the driver. 'Turn on the siren. I'll call the hospital.'

And so we arrived at the hospital with the siren blaring and all other traffic getting out of our way. I thought even then how much this would have amused and delighted her, but, of course, she wasn't aware of it because by then she was barely conscious.

The hospital was great. Everything was ready for us; it took only minutes to get her off the stretcher and on to a bed surrounded by young female doctors, most of whom appeared to be about sixteen years old, but I didn't care, because they seemed to know what they were doing and, anyway, they were soon joined by the blessed Dr Warwicker and, together, they whisked Diana away.

I spent that day and the early evening in the hospital waiting room, drinking lots of coffee and occasionally going outside for a cigarette. I know, I know – smoking will kill you and it will probably kill me. But, God, if you are an addicted smoker, nicotine is a great comfort in times of fear and worry.

Later in the morning Emma joined me, and then so did Bertie, and we hung around, desperate for any scraps of news to be derived from the medical team attending to Diana behind closed doors. They had little to tell us, all of it non-committal.

Samantha, meanwhile, had just that day returned from a skiing holiday in Canada and in the evening was supposed to be interviewing Shirley Williams somewhere in the Midlands. It was part of a series of such events that they did in small theatres all over the country.

We told Mamf what had happened, and she, much cooler than me in a crisis, promptly phoned Dr Warwicker and asked whether, in his opinion, she should carry on with her plans or visit her mother.

'I think,' he said, 'you should visit your mother.' This was the first intimation any of us had of the real gravity of the situation.

Mamf immediately set off for Stevenage, and Emma told Bertie to phone her and tell her that when she arrived she should park at A&E and then call Emma, who would come out and get her.

'Why?' said Mamfie, immediately suspecting the worst. 'Why can't I just come in? What's going on? Where are you, Bertie?'

'Well, I'm, I'm just outside the hospital and . . .'

'Where's everybody else?'

'Oh, they're inside and Mum told me to tell you . . .'

'Why are you outside and they're inside? Don't give me any fucking cryptic messages, Bertie, what's going on? What's happening to your granny? Oh, never mind. I'll be there soon.'

A little after she arrived Dr Warwicker came out to talk to us. It was then that he told us that what Diana was suffering from now was cerebral vasculitis, which was about as serious as it could get. The disease had pretty well abandoned her kidneys and instead attacked the blood vessels in her brain.

By now Diana was sort of conscious, although vague and bewildered, and we were allowed to gather round her bed for a few minutes before she was transferred elsewhere. She was surprised to see us, even more surprised when she learned that we had been around all day. Clearly, she was not at all well, but we were told there was no point in hanging about any longer, so we went home.

The next morning, Samantha and I went to visit her. She was now in intensive care, but awake, apparently not in any imminent danger and pleased to see us, but still somewhat vague.

When she had come home, pretty weak, after the renal vasculitis, the family had tried to persuade her to sleep downstairs in the bedroom that we had added to the house some years earlier. At that time she had refused but now, suddenly, she said: 'I'm coming round to the idea of the Captain Mainwaring Room.'

Mamf and I looked at each other, startled. What the hell was the Captain Mainwaring Room? Captain Mainwaring, played by Arthur Lowe, was the chief character in the BBC sitcom *Dad's Army*. How had he crept into our house?

Eventually it became clear that Diana – who, as she later told us, had no idea why she had called it that – was talking about the downstairs bedroom, now forever known as the Captain Mainwaring Room.

That, however, was the last bit of amusement we were to derive for a very long time.

Later that day they took Diana back to the renal unit, where Dr Warwicker, who knew more about her vasculitis condition than anyone else, could keep an eye on her. The best that could be said about her at that time was that she seemed rather better than she had on the day she was rushed in. But on the Sunday evening, Samantha, Bertie and I were with her when she had another mild fit. Doctors were summoned and again we were told there was nothing we, the relatives, could do and that we should go home.

At nine thirty that night the hospital called me. 'We think you should come in,' they said. Samantha and Emma went in with me. Again, Diana was barely conscious, obviously extremely ill. A registrar was called and said: 'I'm going to give her a brain scan.'

We waited while the scan was done. The news was not good. The blood cells had expanded so much that her brain was almost pressing against her skull. The registrar phoned the Royal Free Hospital, conferring with neurologists, then came to tell us that Diana was to be transferred back to the Intensive Treatment Unit. We sat in the waiting room outside the ITU drinking dreadful coffee from a machine and waiting for good news and getting none, until five o'clock in the morning, when we were told she was unconscious but as comfortable as was possible. Then we went home.

The next several days were much taken up by hospital visits, of which Dee was not aware, because she had fallen into a coma from which she was not to emerge fully for more than a month.

Many times before the vasculitis struck she and I had discussed what we would do if the other became so ill that even if he/she survived there would be permanent brain damage. We both agreed that we would ask the hospital to turn off the life support system. Both of us indeed had written living wills in which we had specified that just such an action should be taken. Neither of us would have wanted to carry on living virtually as vegetables, useless and a burden on our family. And when it became clear that there was a serious possibility that Diana could end up that way, I told her doctors what we had agreed. Mamf was very concerned about this, confiding to Emma that she feared I was so intent that their mother should not survive as a sort of human carrot that I'd have her switched off prematurely.

But I certainly wouldn't have done that and, anyway, when push came to shove . . .

One Friday evening, Samantha, Emma and I were asked to meet Dr Warwicker, Diana's neurologist Dr Bill Wilkinson, and the head of the ITU. Dee's condition had shown no improvement at all, they said. She was still in a coma and not responding to any of the tests. The position seemed hopeless. Perhaps the time had come to turn off the life support?

We discussed it back and forth. If she did wake up, would she certainly be brain-damaged? Well, no, not certainly but . . . In the end, to my and the girls' relief, the doctors agreed to give it until Monday, see what happened.

I cannot possibly begin to tell you what hell that weekend was.

On the Monday we met again. There'd been no improvement. Should we make the final, fatal decision now? The doctors looked at each other. We, the family, watched them anxiously and said nothing. And then, God bless him, Dr Warwicker said: 'Look, I'm going to be away for most of the week, back on Friday. Why don't we leave it till then?'

So it was agreed, and the hell of the weekend stretched into the entire week.

But, come Friday, thank heavens, there were positive signs. She was still in the coma but reacting, if only slightly, to instructions to squeeze someone's finger, or twitching, just a tiny bit, when someone scratched her. The decision to turn off the life support was put on the back burner.

From then on things began slowly to get better, and I do mean slowly. By the time she came out of the coma, May was gone and with it her deadline for completing her latest novel, along with Gordon Brown's Labour Government. They had, she complained, held a general election without consulting her, and what did the Liberal Democrats think they were doing, getting into bed with the bloody Tories? But this was to come later because for a long while she was still confused, still in and out of intensive care. Once, the doctor in charge of the unit that night, desperately short of beds, wanted to send her to a general ward, but Emma, as feisty as her mum and her sister, adamantly refused to let him.

'What if she needs help in the middle of the night?' she asked.

'Well,' he said, 'she'll have a button by her bed. She can press that.'

'Of course she can't!' said Emma. 'In the first place, she's too confused even to know what the button is for and, in the second place, she's too weak to press it anyway.'

Emma won and, in fact, Diana stayed in the ITU for

some days after that, and never was it plain sailing, never could we think that now she could only get better.

Her mental condition was such that for a very long time it was impossible to predict what mood she might be in. Once, Samantha, whom Dee loved, as she did Emma and all the grandsons, better than life itself, was greeted with an angry tirade. And when Mamf pointed out that she'd actually come quite a long way and at some inconvenience to see her, Diana said: 'Well, you shouldn't have bothered, you silly cow.'

Needless to say, Diana remembered none of that the following day.

Another time, I went in with Emma and Bertie. She greeted Bertie warmly. 'How's my grandson?' But all Emma and I got were polite smiles while she talked enthusiastically of Dr Warwicker, with whom she appeared to be in love. After a bit, Emma said: 'Mum, what are our names?'

Diana smiled politely again: 'Oh, do you have to ask such difficult questions?' It was plain that she had no idea who we were and, on the drive home, I said to Emma: 'That's it then. When she comes out she'll have to go and live with Dr Warwicker. He's the only man she recognizes.'

But even that wasn't entirely true. Once, we were with her when a doctor came in to ask her some questions and, after he had gone, she said: 'Isn't he lovely?'

'Who?'

'Dr Warwicker, of course.'

'That wasn't Dr Warwicker.'

'Yes, it was.' But in fact it wasn't.

Her brother Tony drove up from his home in Farnham, Surrey, once or twice a week, and one day he asked if she'd had any other visitors yet. 'No,' she said.

'What about Barry?' he said. 'He came in this morning. He comes in twice a day.'

'No, he doesn't,' she said. 'I never see him.'

One day, she said the only visitor she'd had was Cary Grant, which was odd, because she was never much of a fan of Cary Grant. Actually, she appeared to see him quite a lot, because he seemed to have a habit of running up and down the corridor outside her room while being pursued by a leg of pork. She didn't know why but seemed to accept it as fairly natural and was surprised that anyone should even wonder about it. Later she said the only memories she had of those weeks when she was in a coma or drifting out of it were of Cary Grant and that leg of pork, and of Puccini playing softly on the CD player we'd taken into the hospital for her, having been told that talking to people in comas or playing them their favourite music could help to provoke a reaction.

During all this time our greatest fear was that she would be permanently brain-damaged, something a young doctor warned me was very much on the cards. 'Look,' he said, taking me to one side so the rest of the family wouldn't hear, 'when your wife comes home, you mustn't expect the same woman who came in here.'

Much later, when she'd been home for a while, I told her about this. 'What did you say?' she asked. 'Me?' I told her. 'Well, I said, "Oh, great!" But, unfortunately, they did send the same woman back.' She liked that so much that she kept urging me to repeat it to other people.

But very slowly, very gradually, she got better, although, God, she didn't make it easy on herself. At one time or another she had a tracheostomy and a deeply worrying blood clot in her leg, then contracted MRSA, E. coli, a variety of ominous-sounding -itises and, in short, practically every disease it's possible to catch in hospital. She was rarely in a ward; mostly in an isolation unit because of the danger she posed to other patients. 'You're like bloody Typhoid Mary,' I told her one day as we watched yet another dismal England performance in the football World Cup on the TV in her isolation room. She was really only interested in sport when England were playing, and then she would watch football and even bits of Test matches, though her grasp of cricket was rudimentary at best. She liked rugby union, though, because her brother Roger had been a fine player before and during his Navy days.

When they finally got her out of bed after nearly four months, Diana was so weak that she could barely walk. 'Don't try to do anything,' they told her, 'not even going to the lavatory by yourself. Always call for a nurse.'

Fat chance. Almost the first thing she did was to get out of bed by herself, telling nobody, and make for the loo, whereupon she fell on the bathroom floor and cracked her head open. She was always a bugger for taking advice – always had to do things her own way.

Soon, though, the physiotherapists – or physio-terrorists as they're known to those on whom they practise their dark arts – took her in hand and, twice, she was allowed home for day visits. On both occasions she was so institutionalized, so scared at being away from doctors, nurses and any help she might need if an emergency arose, that she couldn't get back to the hospital fast enough.

But finally, very near the end of July and four months after she had been taken to hospital, came the best day of the entire spring and summer when they said she was now well enough to come home for keeps.

Emma put up 'Welcome Home' bunting and balloons outside our house and I picked Diana up from the hospital and drove her back past Tesco and the police station and the bus station and all the other ugly functional buildings of a post-war new town.

She gazed raptly out of the window and after a while . . . 'Isn't Stevenage beautiful!' she said.

Just for a moment there I thought she really must be brain-damaged after all, but happily it was simply the sheer joy and relief of being alive against all the odds and on her way home.

19

The Worst Day of My Life

A ND SO BEGAN what Diana was to describe as the happiest time of her life. She came home to four months' accumulation of letters, postcards and especially emails from scores of friends, relatives and strangers anxiously asking after her health, singing her praises as a writer and/or offering up prayers for her full recovery. As Emma said, it was a bit like being able to read her own obituaries without having to go through the tiresome business of actually dying. At the very least it was an opportunity granted to very few people, I imagine, to find out while she was still alive just how important she was to so many people and how much she was loved.

I'd had all the downstairs carpets and furniture industrially cleaned, just in case potentially lethal viruses lurked in their depths. Well, you never know. I concentrated on downstairs, because that was where she would have to be for the foreseeable future; there was no way she could even crawl upstairs, let alone walk. So we installed her in the Captain Mainwaring Room; the hospital provided a commode and gizmos to raise and lower the bed and lift her in and out of the bath, and I bought her a wheelchair, which she regarded with disdain.

'Well, I'm not using that for long,' she said, a bold thing to say, considering she was unable to get in and out of bed unaided.

But then, she was remarkably determined. At first, because she was painfully weak after being bedridden for so long, carers came in to wash and bathe her, help her to the loo and (this was what they requested) sleep on a mattress beside her bed in case anything drastic happened in the night.

She liked the carers a lot; well, they were extremely nice women. But she hated sharing her bedroom with such comparative strangers, however helpful they might be, and she was determined to get rid of them as soon as possible. Which is what she did. In, I think, less than a month, as soon as she could get to and from the bathroom by herself, they had gone, with Diana's grateful thanks.

Same with the physioterrorist I'd engaged. He was very good, but he didn't last much more than a month either. 'I think I can manage now,' she said firmly, and he agreed, though he did urge her to make daily use of the exercise bike we kept in what was and pretty well still is the grandsons' playroom.

'Good idea,' she said. 'Yes, I'll do that'; and never went near the thing again.

But that was her way. She could be gloriously infuriating, would rarely take advice unless she had specifically asked for it and usually not even then. The more logical the advice she was given when it contradicted something she was determined to do, the more strongly she resisted it, invariably wearing an expression that irritated me like mad – wide-eyed, unblinking, smiling slightly in a mildly amused way and deeply, deeply stubborn. Mamfie has inherited the look from her.

And she always knew best, especially – and most worryingly – when it came to her own health. Never mind what the doctors advised, she knew better. 'What do they know anyway?' she would enquire, dismissively. Well, actually, a lot more than she did, but she would never admit that.

Nor would she ever admit that she was wrong or, perish the thought, apologize. The closest she ever came to that was after we'd had a row, one she had probably started in the first place, when a couple of hours later she would come up to me, give me a kiss and say: 'I expect you're sorry now.'

She was extremely good at rows: whichever of us was

to blame for an altercation starting, she invariably ended up as the hapless victim. This was because she knew that, while remaining calm herself, she could goad me into losing my temper, and it always worked. Always. I knew exactly what she was up to, tried desperately to keep my cool and failed every time. Her main weapon was to adopt another expression, this time of surprised innocence, as if she couldn't understand what I was getting so het up about, and it was this that annoyed me most, especially when I knew, absolutely knew, that she had been at fault to begin with.

She could also carry a grudge like nobody else. What sent the whole family running for cover were those occasions when, after some altercation the previous evening, she would greet us the next morning with the ominous words: 'I've been thinking about this all night.' That was a sentence to strike terror into the boldest heart, because we knew that she would now be grimly unforgiving for the next couple of hours or however long she felt like it.

Another of her favourite dicta seemed innocuous at first but you'd better listen up or live to regret it. She'd look in on one of us tidying up in the kitchen or wherever, watch for a few moments, then say firmly, 'Now what *I* do in the morning is . . .' – and after that, you knew it had better be done her way or else.

Sometimes the girls would say: 'Dad, I don't know how you put up with her!', to which I would reply: 'I don't either some of the time.' But I did know: it was because I had no idea how I would get along without her. Come to that, I still don't.

As she grew stronger, life returned to something like normal. There were the regular visits to the hospital for check-ups, but these were generally optimistic, especially as all her doctors were amazed that she was still alive. When, late in November, we went to see the neurologist, Dr Wilkinson, he enthusiastically showed her the various brain scans she'd had and said he'd only ever seen three other patients with her condition. 'What happened to them?' Diana asked. 'Oh,' he said, 'one recovered, another died and the third is severely brain-damaged.' Not exactly encouraging, but he seemed very hopeful. When we left, he said: 'Will you come back and see me in six months' time? Not for your sake – for mine.' Diana promised she would, but that, alas, was a promise she was unable to keep.

Meanwhile, the wheelchair had been swiftly banished to the garage and the walking stick she had been using in its place was put aside.

I did all the shopping and much of the cooking, but I enjoy doing both those things, so that was no prob-lem. The real problem was persuading her to stay in the Captain Mainwaring Room, bright and convenient though it was with its en-suite bathroom. Diana had come to dislike it, associating it, understandably enough, with feeling ill, weak and helpless. What she wanted was to return to her own bedroom upstairs, particularly as her study was just along the corridor there. She had gone into hospital leaving a half-written novel tentatively called *Battering Ram*, and she wanted to get on and finish it.

So we compromised. I refused to contemplate the prospect of her struggling up and down stairs several times a day – even walking to the end of the garden was still an effort for her – and insisted that she stay in the Captain Mainwaring Room, where we installed her computer and printer. But then she compromised the compromise. 'I'll work downstairs,' she said. 'But I'll sleep upstairs at night.'

By now the hospital had taken all its gadgets away, and she insisted on taking her nightly bath upstairs as well, which was okay except that, on a couple of occasions, I had to lift her out, despite the installation of various handgrips on the bathroom wall. And that was a worry, because I had resumed the occasional one-man shows I did in various parts of the country. Sometimes this entailed staying overnight at a hotel, and I didn't particularly want to return home one morning to find Diana lying in a bath of cold water, unable to get out, having grimly thought about my absence all night.

Eventually, reluctantly, she agreed not to have a bath unless I or one of the girls was in the house.

And so Christmas approached. Both Mamf and

Emma offered to provide Christmas lunch at their homes, but Diana would have none of it. Everything, she insisted, would be as it was most years: there would be the traditional Norman family Christmas Eve lunch at a local pub, Rick and Christine, their sons Mark and Matt, together with their own families, all attending. Then everyone would come back to our house for champagne, mince pies, sausage rolls, charades and the swapping of presents.

Christmas was very special to Diana; for her, the next one pretty well began the day after Boxing Day. Then she would tour the shops, not looking for stuff for herself but for future presents for other people. And throughout the year numerous catalogues would come through the post, again not because she wanted anything herself but because she was looking for Christmas gifts – books and computer stuff for the children, grandchildren and nieces, and also knives, for unspecified recipients. She was always buying gift packs of table knives with pretty coloured handles, God knows why, because she never seemed to give them away. After her death I discovered that what she called her 'Christmas cupboard' at the top of the stairs was crammed with wrapping paper, Christmas cards, books – and knives, boxes and boxes of knives.

A week or so before what was to be her last Christmas, she arranged to throw a party. As she wrote to one of her electronic penfriends: 'We're having a lunchtime drinks party tomorrow to thank some of the people who were so good to the family while I was poorly. I could have filled the house but Barry, an inhospitable bugger except to those he truly loves, has kept it down to about twenty-five. He doesn't know it but I'm going to say a few words to thank him and the girls for refusing to let the doctors take me off life support. I hate speeches at parties but this one has to be made. After all, the old man has driven me to every clinic, done the shopping, the cooking, bullied me like a despot back on to my feet – and never a word of complaint.'

I rather quibble at the 'inhospitable bugger' bit, although there is a grain of truth in it. I can never understand those who say grandly, 'I love people,' because it's impossible to love people en masse. There are those, Adolf Hitler for instance, who are simply not to be loved. There's a number of people whom I genuinely love, a larger number whom I like or like a lot, and the rest I'm not too bothered about.

But in this instance I restricted the number to twenty-five because that's as many as we could fit, with reasonable comfort, in our sitting room.

We held the party, she made her speech very prettily and we moved on to Christmas Day.

When Diana came out of hospital her hair had thinned. Not very noticeably and not nearly as notice-ably as she believed, but a little. She thought this was down to the chemotherapy she had been given, but her doctors said otherwise. It was, they told her, a result of the extreme severity of her illness and would grow back to normal after a while.

In the meantime, she bought a couple of wigs, a blonde one and another slightly darker and reddish. She liked them a lot, and they looked good on her, except when she was reclining in an armchair watching television, when the wig would either slide up or down the back of her head. Not that she cared. Vanity was never one of her characteristics.

The Christmas Day lunch, overseen by Diana with a little help from her friends, was a triumph, until she poured brandy over the pudding and lit it, whereupon a flame sprang up and singed the front of her wig.

A day or so later I overheard her talking to Margaret Devoil, her hairdresser and guru and just about the only person whose advice she would listen to. Whatever Margaret suggested – a recipe, a place to shop, a place to eat – Diana immediately tried. On the phone she was complaining that 'I burnt my fucking wig on the Christmas pudding,' no doubt leaving Margaret wondering why anyone would possibly want to put a wig on a Christmas pudding.

Now, with hindsight, I believe that somehow Diana knew, or at least feared, that this would be her last Christmas. Hence the party for our friends and her insistence that this time all should be as she remembered Christmas most fondly. If that were so, then I think everything lived up to her expectations. The whole holiday was truly happy and never once was she obliged to think about something all night.

Bertie spent New Year's Eve with us, Emma and Woody, Mamf and her boys being at parties elsewhere. Normally, Diana and I would just have a drink, toast each other, hope the incoming year would be better, even better or at least no worse than its predecessor, and go to bed at a reasonable hour.

But this time Bertie wanted to stay up and see the New Year in, and we stayed with him. I'm glad we did. Stupid, I know, but it's somehow comforting to remember that Diana and I greeted the New Year, her last New Year, together as the clocks chimed.

Early in January I began to realize that her recovery had stopped, that she was growing weaker. She denied it, of course. No, she was fine, she said, feeling better every day. But I knew this wasn't true.

On 20 January 2011, I took her to the Lister Hospital for her regular check-up. Subsequently, she emailed this to one of her fans with whom she kept in regular correspondence:

```
It's been an irritating and time-
wasting week spent mostly at clinics.
My kidney results bleeped a bit (I
think it was all that Christmas eating)
```

and immediately my consultants went
into worry over their pet poodle —
vasculitis is always liable to pop up
again, it appears. So it was back for
more tests — all of them perfectly
normal now. But I did tell them I
wanted to take more exercise — another
bloody thing is that I'm not burning up
the calories as I should and something
has to be done. But I find it difficult
. . . Immediately I was upstairs and in
the hands of my cardiologist, a lovely
Irishwoman I've been under for years —
she'll sort it out, bless her — and
have got a monitor on and a new drug to
take. Don't worry, because I'm not.

This, though, was not the whole truth. On the way
home after the visit to her cardiologist, Mary Lynch, she
said: 'She told me my heart is failing.'

I didn't know what to say; still less did I know what I
could possibly do, except urge her – as I was sure Mary
Lynch had done – not to overdo things, to take greater
care of herself and remind her that she had lived with
this problem for years. But I think we both knew it was
more serious this time.

The following day we had our last row. My fault
somehow, as our rows nearly always seemed to be. She

came to me in the kitchen with her hands full of bits of metal and plastic, saying: 'I'm afraid I knocked your electric shaver off the shelf in the bathroom. Perhaps you can put it together.'

Put it together? It was in more pieces than a giant jigsaw puzzle. What's more, I hadn't had it long and I liked it. So there was much yelling from me, which was what she was waiting for, because now she could see herself as the undeserving victim of my anger and go on the attack.

'The thing was perched precariously on the shelf,' she said.

'No, it wasn't!'

'Yes, it was!'

And so it continued. Within five minutes, it turned out that I was entirely to blame for the fact that she had destroyed my shaver and my wrath was apparently so unreasonable that she phoned Samantha to announce that she was divorcing me.

Mamf passed on the message to Harry: 'Your grandparents are getting divorced.' Harry didn't bother to look up. 'No, they're not,' he said wearily. He'd heard all this stuff before, and Diana loved his response.

The following day, Saturday, I went out to buy myself a new shaver and, as I was driving through Knebworth on my way home, I saw Diana, Emma and Bertie coming out of Coasters, our favourite coffee shop. I waved and parked, Emma and Bertie went about their business, and Diana said: 'Come on, I'll buy you a cup of coffee.' Coming from her, this was an even clearer apology than 'I expect you're sorry now.'

On the Sunday I had to go to Bury St Edmunds to do a show in support of the local theatre. I stayed overnight and, coming home, stopped at a farm shop, where I bought Diana a jar of lemon curd and, because she hated drinking out of thick cups or mugs, a slender coffee mug. They were the last presents I ever bought her. The mug was greatly appreciated, the lemon curd rather less so, because, she said, it wasn't as good as the stuff her mother used to make. She only ate a little of it, and the rest, though long past its use-by date, is still in the fridge, because, I don't know why, I can't bring myself to throw it away.

On the morning of Thursday, 27 January, I had to be up early to be taken to London for a series of interviews. On the Wednesday night while I showered, Diana took a hot-water bottle up to my bed, something she rarely did because I don't normally use hot-water bottles. Why she did it then I have no idea; perhaps she thought it would help me sleep better before the long day that stretched ahead of me.

'Going up and down stairs is getting easier,' she said cheerfully when she had done this, but I knew it wasn't true.

I went to bed and, when she had bathed, she came to me, we kissed and said, pretty much in chorus, as we always did: 'Love you. Sleep well. See you in the morning.'

'You will,' she said.

And those were the last words she ever said to me because, the next morning, I saw her but she didn't see me.

That day I got up at seven o'clock and tiptoed past her room on the way downstairs. She had the bedside light on, her glasses perched on her nose, a novel by Patrick O'Brian (one of her favourite authors) in her hand and she was resting peacefully against the pillows with her eyes closed. I saw no reason to disturb her until, twenty minutes later, the driver phoned to say he was waiting outside our house.

I went back upstairs to give her a wake-up kiss and tell her I was leaving, only this time there was no awakening her. I knew that at once; the cold finality of death is unmistakeable. In fiction – books, plays, movies – people in such circumstances give anguished cries of 'No! Oh, no! Oh, please God, no!' I never used to believe it but now I know it's true. That's exactly what people do.

There was no point in calling an ambulance. Far too late for that. Instead, I called Emma and told her brutally, 'Your mother's dead.' Now I wish I'd found some gentler way of putting it, but in the state I was in, the shock and grief I was feeling, I couldn't think of anything else to say. We both called Mamfie and then I went out to tell the driver I wasn't going anywhere with him that day, but there was no sign of him. God knows whose house he was waiting outside, but it wasn't mine and I never heard from him again.

It was too early to inform our local surgery so Emma dialled 999 to ask to whom she should report her mother's death, and thus the worst day of my life continued.

20

That'll Make the B*****s Cry

To someone who had never before had to report a sudden death via 999 what happened next was kind of weird.

First a paramedic arrived to check the body. I'd expected that. What I had not expected was the arrival soon afterwards and at various intervals of four policemen of increasing rank. 'Well, sudden death,' they said apologetically, 'we have to come.' They didn't say why they had to come but it was pretty clearly to make sure that no foul play was involved.

The very idea that I might have murdered her would have amused Diana enormously. And even at that time of intense grief it amused me, too.

Dutifully, the cops trooped upstairs, each at different times, to examine the corpse, presumably looking for murder weapons, poisons or signs of physical violence, and then, satisfied that they hadn't been greeted by a latter-day Dr Crippen, they all hung around.

The NHS and the police come in for a lot of criticism, but these people couldn't have been politer, more sensitive or more helpful. The paramedic phoned the surgery; the police phoned the undertaker and, when his representatives arrived as well, the whole set-up began to resemble the state-room scene in the Marx Brothers' movie *A Night at the Opera* – more and more people pouring in, and the family – me, daughters, Bertie, Harry and Charlie – totally outnumbered by complete strangers.

We were dazed, shocked, desolate, and the only useful thing we could think of doing was to offer tea or coffee at regular intervals.

Before the undertakers took Diana away the girls and I went upstairs to say our last farewells. She was cold and pale but she still looked lovely, much younger than her seventy-seven years, and remarkably peaceful, as if she had just nodded off, book in hand, which is what I suppose she did. She had died, I'm sure, without any pain and probably without any warning; her failing heart, weakened by the struggle against dreadful illness, simply couldn't take it any more.

We never saw her again.

None of us wanted to visit her in the Chapel of Rest. Whatever undertakers do to make bodies look as good as possible, the result would have ruined the memory of the last time we saw her – as I had seen her so many times – propped up against her pillows and apparently asleep.

Anyway, she hated Chapels of Rest, just as she hated such euphemisms as 'passed away'. As she often said: 'If you're dead, you're dead. Saying you've passed away doesn't make it any better and it certainly doesn't change anything.'

When someone close to you dies there's a lot of rigmarole to go through – probate, the hunting out of bank accounts, investments, wills, whatever. It's tedious but somehow it's good tedious; it stops you brooding too deeply, too much of the time, on what you've lost. Because you're busy seeing lawyers and funeral directors and getting and distributing death certificates and the like, it takes a while before the enormity of that loss begins to dawn. And when realization did come, it could be summed up like this: I had lost my best friend, someone who always had my best interests at heart, who was always there when I needed her, who encouraged me in the good times and comforted me in the bad, the woman I loved to death and beyond. It struck me not immediately but over a period of time that when Diana died a good part of me died, too.

The funeral was great; she'd have loved it. Family, friends, the village turned out in force. Both the girls spoke; so did all three boys, Bertie claiming, probably with some justification, that thanks to the hours his granny had spent teaching him to spell he was quite likely the only person in the church who knew how to spell *diarrhoea* correctly.

I said nothing; I couldn't. As with my parents' funerals, I knew that if I stood up and opened my mouth I would immediately break down into uncontrollable grief, and that's pretty bloody embarrassing for all concerned at a funeral.

Anyway, Mamf pretty well said it for all of us:

It is, as Mum would have said, 'a bit of a bugger' when your best friend, heroine and closest confidante also happens to be your own mother, because when they leave you the sense of loss is so much greater than it would have been if she hadn't been quite so extraordinary and I hadn't loved her quite so much. But then she was exceptional.

She was exceptionally kind and generous, all her many, many friends would attest to that; she was unusually talented, a legion of literary fans and book sales would attest to that, too; but she also had this incredible breadth of knowledge and wisdom. Those of us fortunate enough to have been recipients of her wisdom – whether we liked it or not and there were times, I must be honest, when I did not – inevitably buckled down and benefited from it.

A friend of mine, who, like everybody else, adored her, spent time trying to analyse her extraordinary charisma. 'It's like she has the gravitational pull of a dark star,' he said, and she did. Many times I amused myself watching new people she'd taken a shine to blunder into her orbit succumbing inevitably to the Diana Norman charm, and I'd say to myself: 'Oh dear, New Person, that's it, you're hooked for life now.' And after that they would be taken on and encouraged to do things with their lives that they'd never thought were possible and she would provide the support and wherewithal for them to be done.

Her great reward for all her gifts was that she died the most contented, happy, fulfilled and loved person I've ever met.

If she had a fault it was that she always left everywhere too early; there'd come a time during an evening out when she'd put her handbag on her lap, smile seraphically around at the people before her – carefully avoiding eye-contact in case a conversation prolonged her exit – and then say: 'Well, my darlings,' and she would go. As in life, in death she left too soon, but then, as Emma said, it was always going to be too soon.

The service was conducted by an old family friend, the Revd Richard Syms, who used to be our vicar and who combines being a clergyman with a second career as a very good professional actor.

Diana, who loved routine and was very organized in arranging her affairs, had left clear instructions as to which hymns and why were to be played at the service.

So at one point Richard announced: 'The next hymn is "Abide With Me" because, as Diana said, "That'll make the buggers cry at my funeral." ' And it did. Well, as Eric Morecambe would have put it, 'Always a belter was that,' and it was hard to tell which was the louder, the singing or the sobbing.

The wake was held in a marquee in our front garden, where we ate curry, which Diana loved, and swapped stories about her. The girls and I had actually invited about eighty people; well over one hundred turned up, but – loaves and fishes – there was more than enough food and drink for everyone and all agreed that it was the best funeral they'd ever been to, which I suppose was a kind of compliment, and one she would have appreciated.

Late in the afternoon of that bright, sunny February day, it was all over. The guests and the caterers had gone, and there was just the immediate family facing the knowledge that life had to go on and knowing that it would never be the same again. It would never, ever, be remotely the same again. As I wrote in an article about her in the *Daily Mail*, 'I can't begin to express the agony in those words.'

The only great consolation is that in those last six months she was happier than she had ever been and she and I were closer than we had ever been. Quite often she would come to me for no reason at all, give me a kiss and say, 'I love you.' And I'd just grin and say, 'Well, I love you, too,' and we both knew it was so.

21

An Empty Chair

ONE THING I'VE discovered about Diana since she died is that she was bloody untidy. As she used to scurry about the house clearing up bits and pieces, she would blame me for it. 'Look at the mess you've made!' And the accusation was so forcible that I would apologize.

But now that I live alone, the house is tidier than it's ever been. No longer is there a trail of those lipstick-smeared tissues that, like one of the Babes in the Wood, she would leave all over the place as if they were a sort of trail to help her back to where she started. Her coat pockets, as the girls and I discovered, were full of more tissues, old cigarette packets, empty disposable lighters, credit-card receipts from way back and bits of rubbish she'd picked up on the green outside our house and forgotten to put in the dustbin.

She was also, in her private life, remarkably disorganized. I couldn't begin to count the number of times when, just as we were about to go out, she would say, 'Where's my purse?' Or handbag, or credit card, or mobile, or car keys. And then a row would develop with me asking, reasonably I thought, why she couldn't leave the damn things in the same place every time and she telling me to shut up because she was trying to think where she had last seen whatever we were searching for this time and wondering whether it was in Waitrose or the Co-op, before it finally came to light in the fridge, or somewhere equally improbable.

The memory of such occasions, irritating as they were at the time, took on a sharp poignancy now that she was gone. In moments of loneliness I'd have given anything to have her back wildly accusing me of having moved her car keys, which was why she couldn't find them.

The wife of an old family friend died soon after Diana, and some time later when I was talking to her husband on the phone I asked how he was getting along. 'Okay,' he said. 'I'm coping and trying not to feel sorry for myself.'

And that's just what I was doing – coping and trying not to feel sorry for myself. Grief, I've discovered, is a selfish emotion. I mourn not for Diana, because she was spared all the things she feared – pain, the recurrence of vasculitis, another long spell in hospital, or Alzheimer's, which she was convinced would strike her, though there was never any sign of it. Her death, indeed, was one I would happily choose. No, I mourn for Samantha and Emma, Bertie, Harry, Charlie and myself and for the loss we are suffering.

But feeling sorry for myself is sometimes hard to resist when I come back to an empty house and look at the now empty armchair where she used to wait for me no matter how late I returned from whatever event I'd been attending, because she wouldn't go to bed until she knew I was safely home. And it creeps up on me, too, when I'm watching some rubbish on television and want to turn to her and say, 'Why are we wasting our time on this crap?' Sometimes I do find myself saying it to that empty armchair.

So as an alternative to turning into some snivelling, self-pitying wreck, the only thing to do was to keep busy, and I did that by continuing to write for the *Radio Times*, as I have done for more than twenty years, sometimes for the *Daily Mail* and other papers and magazines, and turning up occasionally on radio or television shows to pontificate grandly about the movies.

Then there was my so-called lecture tour, which I'd started doing a couple of years after I left Sky and gave up the day job. Clive Conway, who arranges such things for the likes of Shirley Williams, Tony Benn, Michael Portillo and Trevor McDonald, approached me to ask whether I fancied doing a one-man show, appearing in small theatres all over the land.

Did I fancy it? Well, not much really. I have no problem talking to cameras and microphones, because you have their undivided, silent attention. They don't keep coughing or fidgeting or talking to their neighbours or nodding off and snoring. But the prospect of real, live audiences kind of terrified me.

'What would I have to do?' I asked, and Clive said, Oh, it was quite simple – just talk about your life and career for forty-five minutes then, after a drinks break (doubtless much needed by the audience), do a question and answer session for another forty-five minutes.

The Q&A bit didn't bother me; I'd done that numerous times since the mid-seventies when, out of the blue, the president of the Oxford Union asked me to take part in a debate. I was thrilled and hugely flattered and proudly told Alan Coren about it the same day when I went to one of the lunches he gave as editor of *Punch*.

He, an Oxford graduate himself, turned pale. 'Christ, you're not going to do it, are you?' he said. I asked why not. 'Well, think about it,' he said. 'You're a busy man. You won't have time to write your speech till you're on the train at Paddington, but those little shits will have been polishing their aphorisms for weeks. They'll wipe the floor with you.'

I knew he was right, so I declined the invitation and

have ever since refused to take part in debates. A while later I said as much to the president of the Cambridge Union, who had proffered a similar invitation, and he said: 'Okay, come and do a Q&A session instead.' This seemed much less terrifying, so I accepted and it turned out pretty well. Since then I'd frequently gone down the Q&A route at Oxford and Cambridge, both at the Unions and individual colleges, as well as places like Durham University and Trinity College, Dublin. Q&A I was fine with, but the other stuff Clive was talking about . . .

Never had I attempted in a theatre or anywhere else except TV and radio to hold an audience's attention for anything like forty-five minutes, other than in Q&A sessions. Alone, in an armchair on a stage – who the hell would want to come and listen to me? I certainly wouldn't.

But after a lot of anguished thought I decided to give it a go, just to see if I could carry it off. My first date was in Swindon, and I spent a week writing my speech, learning it by heart and practising it. Diana wanted to come with me on the night, but I wouldn't let her; if humiliation loomed ahead, as I was gloomily sure it would, I didn't want her there to see it.

In the end it was pretty successful, although it nearly didn't happen at all. About an hour away from Swindon on the M4 I had a panic attack. I can't do this, I thought; I'll pull on to the hard shoulder, phone the theatre and tell them I can't make it because my car has broken down/I've been attacked by terrorists/overcome by food poisoning/had a heart attack/whatever. But then I thought, No, if I chicken out of this, I'll never have the guts to do anything new ever again. So I carried on and, to my huge relief, the audience seemed happy and so did Clive, who had dropped by to monitor the show.

Then, in the spring of 2011, I was offered something else that would help keep me occupied. One Friday evening as I was sitting alone at home, the phone rang and the voice on the other end said: 'Is that broadcasting legend Barry Norman?'

Warily, I said: 'Yeeees.'

'Well, this is broadcasting legend Chris Tarrant. How would you like to be president of the Lord's Taverners?'

I said: 'Come off it, Chris. You're taking the piss. This is a joke, right?'

He said: 'No! I'm serious. We need you. We can't get any other bugger to take it on.'

Well, that's how I like to remember the conversation, anyway, and I thought: if an offer's put to you in such flattering terms you've really got to consider it. So I did. I considered it all weekend and came to the conclusion that I couldn't do it.

There were lots of reasons, paramount among them the fact that I'd never aspired to such lofty office. I'd joined the Taverners because I wanted to play cricket alongside real cricketers, and I'd done that. And when my playing days were over I turned to umpiring Taverners' matches alongside men I now regarded as old friends, men like John 'Sport' Price, the former England and Middlesex fast bowler, and the late Mike Denness, who had captained England and played for Kent and Essex. I saw myself as a humble foot soldier in the Taverners' ranks and was content in that capacity.

So on the Monday morning I started writing a letter to John Ayling, the chairman of the club, expressing gratitude for the offer but reluctantly declining on the grounds of age, lack of time, being too busy and any other excuse that came to mind. I was halfway through it when John rang me. I started telling him what I was doing and why and he said: 'Oh, come on – it's not that demanding. There are only six or seven events you really have to attend as president.'

I said: 'Really? What are they?'

He listed them. I looked in my diary and found I was actually clear on all of the dates he mentioned. 'Well,' I said, 'if that's so, maybe I could manage to—'

'Great,' he said. 'You're the new president. Congratulations.'

I said: 'But you're absolutely sure, are you – just six or seven events?'

'Yes!' he said. 'Six or seven.'

What a bloody liar.

I'd only been in the post a couple of months before I'd done at least six or seven events, none of them among those John had listed. One of them was on Father's Day, our annual home game against the Emirates Airline on a ground at Windsor, just below the castle. The Duke of Edinburgh turned up, because he's our Patron and Twelfth Man, though I must say he's pretty invisible in the latter capacity. I can't remember any time when I've seen him carrying drinks, a spare bat or a fresh pair of gloves to the batsmen, still less jogging around at fine leg while the fast bowler goes off for a much-needed pee. Still, he turned ninety that year so I suppose we ought to cut him some slack.

At lunch, Chris Tarrant asked him if he'd had any Father's Day cards that morning. 'No,' said the Duke, scornfully. I don't know whether the scorn was directed at the idea that his children would bother to send such things or at the commercial phoniness of Father's Day itself. The latter would be my bet.

I was, in fact, the Taverners' president by default. In 2011, the job should have gone to Chris Cowdrey, the former Kent and England captain and son of Colin, but, for various reasons, each of which was carefully explained to me several times and which I never did understand, he was unable to take it on at the time. But I didn't mind that and was happy to keep the seat warm for him.

In any event, it wasn't a particularly arduous job.

Mostly it involved attending cricket matches (never a hardship for me) and fund-raising lunches and dinners, where I was called upon to speak from time to time during the meal. Since I don't much like public speaking except at events, such as my one-man show, where the audience has turned up specifically to hear me and can therefore be assumed to be on my side, this was a bit of a downer. On the other hand, the fact that I had to get on my feet every now and then meant that I didn't get pissed.

One of the most memorable evenings was the Fast Bowler's Dinner attended by nearly a thousand people because for the first – and almost certainly the last – time twenty-three of the greatest fast bowlers of the last few decades came from all over the world to assemble together in one room at the same time. There they were – Glenn McGrath, Michael Holding, Courtney Walsh, Curtly Ambrose, Bob Willis, Garfield Sobers . . . Well, I guess you have to be a cricket lover to understand what an awesome spectacle it was. The diners certainly did; I think we raised more than £100,000 that night.

The climax of my year was a week-long visit to Dubai, where the Taverners played two games against the Emirates Airline, who flew us out there as their guests. We had a pretty good team that included Chris Adams (Sussex and England), Murray Goodwin (Sussex and Zimbabwe), Vikram Solanki (Worcestershire and England), Gareth Batty (Worcestershire,

Surrey and England), Neil Smith (Warwickshire and England), Neal Radford (Worcestershire and England) and a handy fast bowler in Steve Kirby of Somerset. Okay, some of the guys were past their best, but others were still playing first-class cricket. The result should have been a doddle for us, but in the first match the Emirates thrashed us out of sight, hugely to the delight of Sir Maurice Flanagan, who founded the airline from scratch and is probably the world's biggest cricket nut.

Maurice has since retired and the Taverners no longer play the airline home and away. But is it a coincidence that during his time in charge most of the Emirates Airline team also played for the United Arab Emirates in international matches? I don't think so. I'm not suggesting that Maurice picked his pilots on the basis of their batting or bowling averages, but I do feel you had a better chance of a job with the airline if you could play a bit.

The second match we won, much to the disgust of the world's biggest cricket nut, who had watched every ball of both games from the boundary edge, usually by himself, because he didn't want idle chit-chat to disrupt his concentration.

The airline has its own cricket ground, an emerald-green oasis surrounded by scrubby desert. The local golf clubs are much the same – immaculate, well-watered fairways and greens surrounded by a foreboding expanse of greyish, hard-packed sand.

Altogether, Dubai is a bizarre place, 'a twenty-second century city', as my fellow Taverner Roger Oakley described it. It's a city of six-lane highways teeming with traffic and a miniature Manhattan skyline in which the skyscrapers are an eclectic blend of Western and Arabic architecture. It seems to be a popular holiday resort for the likes of overpaid Premier League footballers whose private lives are not all they might be and who want to keep out of the British media spotlight for a bit, but it's not a place I'd choose for a holiday.

For a start, it's very expensive. Yes, okay, as privileged guests we had a great time; we stayed at the Meydan, a five-star hotel built right beside the racetrack of the same name. We were wined and dined by golf clubs and the Dubai equivalent of the Jockey Club, and one evening I sat on my balcony, cold beer in hand, watching Frankie Dettori win yet another race.

But, another night, a whole bunch of us led by Mike Gatting went out to dine at his favourite Dubai restaurant, where my meal – steak and chips, no more – cost me fifty quid. It was a fillet steak, admittedly imported from America, and the knife just slid through it, but £50 for a six-ounce steak and chips? Others, hungrier than I and ordering bigger slabs of meat, were paying £70 or £80. No doubt a London banker, casually pocketing his £1 million bonus for successfully over-seeing yet another drop in his company's profits, might wonder what on earth I'm complaining about.

But what I'm saying is that, unless you're a London banker or a Premier League footballer, Dubai is an expensive place.

One evening I was invited on to a TV chat show and, just before I went on, the producer said: 'Word of advice – don't mention sex, pork or alcohol. Big Muslim influence here.' This, of course, was counter-productive because immediately I started concocting sentences in which I could include all three.

'Don't do that,' he said, 'or the police will come and arrest me. They don't like us letting people talk about sex, pork or alcohol on television.' Not a bit like home, where no chat show would last five minutes without mention of sex or alcohol, though not necessarily pork.

Back in London, there were two more events – the Umpires' Dinner and the Spring Lunch at Lord's, where I handed over to Chris Cowdrey – and then I was done, yesterday's man.

The Umpires' Dinner is a curious event; nobody knows why it is so called and, apart from me, there wasn't an umpire in sight. Prince Edward was there as guest of honour and, as president, I was supposed to greet him at the hotel entrance, but, I dunno, I got caught up talking to riff-raff like Chris Tarrant and David Frost and by the time I set off the prince was already halfway up the stairs to the dining room.

'I'm so sorry,' I said.

'What for?'

'Well,' I said, 'I should have met you at the door, bowing and scraping and tugging my forelock.'

He grinned. 'Don't worry,' he said, 'I'm a big boy now. I can find my own way.'

At the end of the evening we asked where he was off to next – hitting the discos perhaps, like Prince Harry? He was horrified. 'God, no,' he said. 'Harry's way out of my league.'

The Royal Family, apart from the Queen, come in for a lot of undeserved flak from the press but – speak as you find – in my experience, they're a charming, courteous bunch and entertaining to be with. I've only met the Queen on formal occasions, but the others I've encountered over the years – Prince Philip, the Prince of Wales, Princess Anne and Prince Edward – are easy to chat to and show a sense of humour that the newspapers rarely mention.

On which subject, I once spent a strange evening with Princess Anne. It was towards the end of my time on the *Daily Mail*, and that night she was to be shown round the building and introduced to selected members of the staff – writers and executives, me among them. The evening began with dinner in a very discreet Knightsbridge hotel, where of the *Mail* contingent only the chairman Vere Harmsworth (later Lord Rothermere) and the editor Arthur Brittenden were invited to sit at the princess's table.

Later, we all went back to the *Mail* and, while Arthur

and Vere (genially known on the editorial floor as 'Mere') showed their guest the building, the rest of us gathered in the editor's office for drinks. Well, what with an excellent and well-lubricated dinner and the stuff we knocked back in Arthur's office, we weren't at our most sober by the time the princess rejoined us. I certainly wasn't, which perhaps explains why I decided all of a sudden that of all the people in the room the one she most obviously wanted to talk to was me. Filled with alcohol-fuelled self-confidence, I felt this was perfectly understandable; I was clearly the most attractive and interesting person present. Any good-looking young woman, I felt sure, would want to talk to me. So I stepped up to the plate and proceeded pretty well to monopolize her for the rest of the evening. What we talked about I have no idea, although I do remember admiring the dress she was wearing and asking her where she bought it because I wanted to buy one just like it for Diana. The curious thing is that, apart from refusing to tell me where she got her clothes, she didn't seem to mind my attentions; indeed, she seemed amused and smiled and laughed a lot, very possibly I suppose because she had never before been accosted by a commoner quite so amiably pissed as I was and rather enjoyed the novelty.

At midnight when the visit ended, I poured myself into a chauffeur-driven car and went home. Already vague doubts were surfacing about my behaviour, and the next morning when I awoke with the most God-awful hangover and alcoholic remorse, these doubts became vivid. I simply couldn't face going into the office and called in sick. Nor was the following morning much better; the doubts and the guilty conscience were still eating me but now there was no excuse for not going to work. I was hoping just to slink in and hide in my office, but the first person I encountered was the fashion editor, Sandy Fawkes, smiling at me in a sort of meaningful way.

'Enjoy yourself the other night?' she asked.

'Oh yes,' I said, with such nonchalance as I could muster. 'Very nice. I, er, I seem to remember spending quite a lot of time chatting to the princess.'

Sandy grinned evilly. 'Chatting to her? Chatting *to* her? I wouldn't say chatting *to* her – more like chatting her up.'

Oh, my God! I went to my desk and wrote a note to the editor. 'Dear Arthur,' I began, and went on to thank him fulsomely for inviting me to such an enjoyable event. I put it in the out-tray and waited for his response. Several hours later it came: 'Dear Norman, One day I hope the princess will find it in her heart to forgive you. I cannot. Yours sincerely, Arthur Brittenden.' Oh, my God! Now, surely, I was in trouble. But, happily not, because when next I saw Arthur he grinned wickedly at me and hoped my head felt better.

I have never since met the Princess Royal, as she now

is, so whether she did forgive me I don't know. I hope so; even more I rather hope she enjoyed the occasion; but either way it doesn't matter because, anyway, I'm a royalist. In part, as I explain to my friends who aren't, that's because if Britain were a republic we would almost certainly have had to suffer years of President Margaret Thatcher and later President Tony Blair, at which point I rest my case. Besides, as a CBE, I know that the Queen regards me as 'trusty and well-beloved' and I have a certificate to prove it.

In my farewell speech at the Spring Lunch at Lord's, I explained how I had tried to set about the job once it sank in that I was indeed the Taverners' president, that I was The Man, that I had the Power, and I started looking around to see how other men of power behaved, seeking a role model. As I told the audience, my first choice – obviously – was the former Italian prime minister Silvio Berlusconi but, when I discovered that the girls at the Lord's Taverners HQ weren't nearly as keen on bunga-bunga as Berlusconi's totty, I gave that up.

Sepp Blatter, the president of FIFA, was my next choice, my argument being that I was deeply impressed by his firm intention to clean up all the corruption in FIFA – just as soon as it was convenient for everybody, of course. I determined to do the same with the Taverners but, since I couldn't find the remotest sign of corruption anywhere, I abandoned that, too, and just ambled along in my own way.

What, if any, impact I had as president I have no idea, but my pickled onions were a huge success.

My career as a purveyor of pickled onions to the discerning was my first, and almost certainly my last, venture as a businessman, and it came about, as much in my life has done, more or less by accident. My mother used to make the most wonderful pickled onions, using a recipe she had inherited from her own mother, which took it way back into the nineteenth century. When Mum died, I carried on the family tradition, adhering faithfully to her recipe. Diana and the girls liked pickled onions so I made them quite often and gave jars of them to Samantha and Emma.

Some time in 2004, Emma gave a supper party for our mutual friends John and Delith Wringe, who live about a hundred yards away from her. During the course of the meal she brought out a jar of my onions and handed them around. John took one, crunched into it and so I am told – because I wasn't there at the time – underwent an epiphany. It was like St Paul on the road to Damascus. 'These,' he said, 'are the best pickled onions I've ever tasted. They've got to be marketed.' Apparently, he knew of what he spoke, for he is an aficionado of pickled onions, a man who can eat a jar of them unaccompanied by anything else.

The next day, Emma told me of his reaction. 'Oh, yes,'

I said. 'Quite late at night, was it? Couple of bottles of wine consumed?'

'Well, yes,' she said. So, while glad that John had enjoyed the things, I forgot all about it until John himself turned up, enthusiastically repeating what he had said the night before. 'They absolutely have to be marketed,' he said.

Now, marketing pickled onions, or anything else come to that, is not exactly one of my skills but, fortunately, it didn't matter, because John is one of the best marketing and advertising men around. 'Leave it to me,' he said, so I did.

Over the next eighteen months or so he arranged meetings with various manufacturers and, in the end, we threw in our lot with Bennett Opie, an old-established family firm in Sittingbourne, Kent, partly because, among other things, it makes a variety of excellent pickles and partly because we both liked the boss, William Opie, and his right-hand man, Paul Fox.

And so, in 2007, Barry Norman's Pickled Onions, later to be followed by Barry Norman's Pickled Shallots (less spicy but just as tasty), found their way into Tesco, Waitrose and Sainsbury's. Regrettably, Tesco dropped them when the recession hit and have not so far taken them up again, but they are still to be found in Waitrose, Sainsbury's and various other places.

Lending my name and my/Mum's/Granny's recipe to a couple of commercially pickled vegetables – albeit the most delicious you can buy – doesn't exactly put me in the Paul Newman bracket, nor has it made John and me rich. But then, we never expected it would. From the start, we regarded the venture as something to do for fun, something quite unlike anything either of us normally does, and that's how it has turned out.

Just before the Spring Lunch prior to my anointment as president of the Taverners, John Ayling asked me, pretty much as a joke, to donate a jar of onions for the auction, thinking it might raise thirty or forty quid, the Taverners being remarkably generous people in their support of charity.

It went for £800. I kept shouting: 'You can get them cheaper at Waitrose and Sainsbury's!' but it made no difference. At a later event, two more jars were bought for £800 apiece; at a dinner in Dubai, the cricketer Neil Smith paid £850; and at my farewell Spring Lunch, Chris Tarrant broke all existing records by forking out £950.

In Dubai, Neil opened the jar as soon as he had bought it and handed it round the table. He himself ended up eating only one, which is probably worthy of a place in the *Guinness Book of Records* as the most expensive pickled onion in the history of the world.

22

Living without Dee

S O WHERE ARE we now?

Well, at the time of writing, a Canadian company has taken an option on the right to make either films or a TV series of Diana's four Ariana Franklin novels. In Hollywood, my ex-brother-in-law, Bernie Williams, is likewise trying to set up films or TV series based on her Makepeace trilogy; and in Dublin, an Irish producer, Noel Pearson, is investigating the possibility of making a film version of *Terrible Beauty*. Of course, the chances are that none of these will come off; in the past, both Diana and I have had the BBC and other companies take up options on our books, and nothing has ever happened. But that's the nature of the entertainment industry and I'm sure numerous other writers have had similar experiences. It's a crapshoot really.

Nevertheless, Diana would have been thrilled to

know that so much interest was being taken in her books and it's sad that none of this happened when she was still around to enjoy it. She, even more than I, would have been pessimistic about the possibility of anything ever appearing because, although she was rightly proud of her work, she was far too modest to appreciate how good it really was, but she would have revelled in the fun of it and the attention she was getting.

As for me, I'm still writing articles and film reviews, occasionally pontificating about the movies in interviews and doing my one-man show from time to time, although a few years back I changed the format. Now, instead of reminiscing in the first half, I discuss the making of a number of classic films. I've done this all over England, Scotland and Wales, once in southern Spain and many times in both parts of Ireland, to audiences varying from a few score in more remote places to several hundred in others. I reckon I must be running out of small theatres by now.

One thing I did not do was finish Diana's half-completed novel, *Battering Ram*. Her publishers were eager for someone to do it, but it would have been beyond me. She had her own distinct style of writing, entirely different from mine. What to do? Both the family and Helen Heller were reluctant to hand the job over to some outsider. So Mamf volunteered to take it on. Her mother and I – particularly her mother – had been urging her to write for some time and, gallantly, she shouldered the task, including a good deal of necessary research, and did it magnificently. Yes, well, I would say that, wouldn't I, being a proud father, but don't just take my word for it. Hard-headed business-people have been equally impressed not only by the way she worked out the plot (Diana had left no notes) but equally by the way it's impossible to tell from the writing itself where her mother left off and Mamf began. If it hasn't been published by the time I finish this, I urge Diana's fans to watch out for it in the near future under its new title of *Winter Siege*. And no, I don't care if that last sentence comes under the heading of 'product placement'.

In addition to completing the novel, Mamf, like me, is continuing to tour small theatres, where she conducts interviews and Q&A sessions with Shirley Williams and, mostly, Tony Benn.

As for Emma, some years ago she decided that what she really wanted to do was teach. She already had a BA in history; now she enrolled at the University of Hertfordshire to qualify as a teacher of English and media studies, after which she was taken on at a comprehensive school in Stevenage. She was (again, I would say this, wouldn't I?) a natural at it; her various forms' results in GCSEs and A levels were excellent and many of her pupils posted messages on Facebook declaring her to be 'the best teacher I've ever met'. But for no other than purely local administrative reasons, that school was already due to close down and the one she moved to afterwards was not nearly such a happy place.

It often seems to me that almost the first thing any government, whatever its political colour, does on taking office is screw up the state education system, invariably by messing about with the exams kids take at sixteen and eighteen. But they always miss the point. It's not the exams that are the problem but the structure itself. What state education needs is more schools, more and better qualified and better paid teachers, and smaller class sizes. At Emma's second school, some classes were so large that there weren't enough chairs to go round and kids were perching on the edge of other kids' desks. Discipline throughout was hard to maintain, largely because the sanctions at teachers' disposal are pretty pathetic, and partly because parental support or even interest was more or less non-existent.

The trouble is, of course, that putting such matters to rights would cost money. Much easier and cheaper for a government to change the exam system and pretend it's achieved something. Those who rearranged the deckchairs on the *Titanic* probably had a similar feeling of accomplishment.

Meanwhile, the grandsons are all in full-time education and hoping to go to university and, yes, I know – this bit is beginning to read like one of those awful round-robin letters people send their friends at

Christmastime, telling them what the entire family has been up to. Well, can't be helped.

I have a photograph of Diana, her favourite, propped up beside the fireplace in the sitting room, and I talk to it frequently, filling her in on the events of the day and occasionally cursing her soundly for having died before me. I rarely visit her grave, because I have no feeling that she is there. That worried me for a while and I mentioned it to our clergyman friend Richard Syms. 'Don't worry, it's quite understandable,' he said reassuringly. 'Only her mortal remains are in the grave, her spirit is elsewhere.'

And so it is. I still feel her presence in every room in the house, which is why I don't intend to leave it, though it's more than big enough for just me. A small bungalow or a flat would be more convenient, but there I would truly feel alone.

The fact is that I miss her desperately. We all do, and talk about her frequently. If I bore my friends rigid with my reminiscences of her, I really don't care. Harv, the husband of Lacey in the American TV series *Cagney and Lacey*, was always telling his wife: 'You are my life, Mary Beth,' and every time he said it Diana would turn to me accusingly and say: 'Why don't you ever say that to me?'

To which I would reply: 'Okay – "You are my life, Mary Beth." Happy now?'

But the fact is she was my life, someone whose love

and support I could depend upon whatever the circumstances. In local newspapers there are frequent photographs of elderly couples celebrating their golden anniversary, beaming and holding hands, and they're always quoted along the lines of 'Fifty years together and never a cross word.' To which I can only say: what the hell kind of marriage was that?

The only person with whom I could live for any length of time with never a cross word would be someone for whom I felt total indifference. Diana and I had many a cross word. We could both be infuriating, aggravating, petulant, angry, argumentative, opinionated and pretty well intolerable at times, but I couldn't have done without her and I don't think she could have done without me.

There is no single recipe for a long and happy marriage, but what worked for us was that we always gave each other space. We both loved good books, plays and movies, but we didn't necessarily share all of each other's interests nor did we feel obliged to pretend we did. She loved sailing, I didn't; I loved cricket, she didn't; so she would go off to her yacht and I would go to Lord's and we'd both be happy. The idea that we had to do absolutely everything together would have driven us both to distraction.

When we went out for a meal, just the two of us, we would each take a book and read while we ate, because we both felt that eating, drinking and reading are three of the four greatest pleasures in life and the only ones you can do in public. Other couples in the restaurant, many of them staring silently and moodily over each other's shoulders, would no doubt look at us and think: 'God, their marriage must be even worse than ours.' But that, too, would be to miss the point. Once again, it was a matter of giving each other space. If we had something to say we said it; if not we read and the silence was warm and companionable.

The thing is that through all the ups and downs, the stand-up rows and reconciliations, the one element that never entered our marriage was boredom, in part because, although I felt I knew her as well as it was possible to know anyone, she could always surprise me and has continued to do so even after her death. We never read each other's letters or emails unless invited to, and it wasn't until I started researching this book, more than a year after she died, that I read the mail she had received from other people.

The result was mildly astonishing, because I came across a small hoard of passionate love letters and poems sent to her during the latter part of her life by an octogenarian. Some of the letters were fifteen pages long, mostly stuff about himself but dotted with powerful terms of endearment. God knows what she wrote to him in reply, though I have absolutely no reason to believe that the passion was reciprocated. I knew she was fond of him and of his wife, both of them respected and moderately well-known writers. But I liked them, too, though had I known what he was writing to my own wife I might have been a little less hospitable when they came to our house. I certainly wouldn't have let the amorous little bugger get pissed that time on my best Calvados.

Diana, of course, never said a word to me about this correspondence or indeed any other deeply personal letters or emails she might have received. For all I know, she was a veritable femme fatale, constantly pursued by lovelorn admirers, in which case, good luck to her. None of it ever adversely affected me or my relationship with her – but it just goes to show that you never know everything about anybody else, no matter how long you may have been together, and that's okay. People are entitled to have their own close secrets.

And then there's another thing: I could never work out quite how her mind worked.

We each used to do the *Times* cryptic crossword puzzle every day, starting off competitively but then invariably arriving at a point where neither of us could do any more. Then we'd compare notes and, again invariably, discover that exactly the same clues had defeated both of us. There would follow a period of intense reflection until suddenly she would say: 'I think the answer to two down is so-and-so.'

I'd consider it and, still baffled, ask: 'Why?'

A shrug. 'I dunno. I just think it is.'

So I'd return to the clue, working backwards from the answer she had provided, and after much laborious thought realize she was right, though I would never have solved it without her help.

'Why am I right?' she would ask, and I'd tell her.

'Oh, really? Aren't I clever?'

I don't mean that as a generalization about how men and women's minds work differently. It's specific to Diana and me. She was intuitive in a way that I'm not.

I still do the *Times* crossword puzzle, and even complete it from time to time, but it's a lot more difficult without her help, and I miss that. I also miss what, at the time, seemed quite irritating things about her. For instance . . .

Often of an evening we'd be watching television, and she'd say: 'Got a fag?'

I, knowing what was to come, would reply: 'Yes, thanks. Plenty.'

A brief pause, then, impatiently . . . 'Well, give one to me.'

'Where are yours?'

'Upstairs.'

'Why are they upstairs?'

Impatiently again: 'Because I left them there.' Another pause, then the impatient tone turned to a piteous one. 'You're not going to send me all the way upstairs to get them, are you?'

I would give her a cigarette.

Later, this time with an imperious click of the fingers: 'Fag.'

I would ignore her until . . . 'I said, "Fag!"'

'Yes, I know you did. What about "Please"?'

Much sighing and exasperated rolling of eyes. 'Pleeeease!'

I would throw her another cigarette. Then more clicking of fingers. 'Lighter!'

'Where's yours?'

'I dunno. I can't find it.' It was almost certainly somewhere in the folds of her armchair, but she couldn't be bothered to look for it. So I would throw her my lighter, and so it would go on, until we both went up to bed. We always did our pleasure reading in bed – the books we wanted to read rather than the ones we had to read – usually with the accompaniment of a cup of tea and a cigarette.

'Fag,' she would say.

'What? Smoke your own bloody fags.'

'Can't – they're downstairs.'

'How the hell did they get downstairs? Three hours ago they were up here and you certainly didn't come and fetch them.'

'I don't know, but that's where they are – downstairs.'

It was a mischievous game she played, largely because she knew it irritated me, although sometimes she'd take it a bit too far, when, at the end of a day, she'd look at my cigarette packet and say: 'God, look how many fags you've smoked.' Then, smugly, she would show me her own packet. 'And see how few I've had.'

'But you've been smoking mine all night!' It didn't matter; the evidence suggested that I'd smoked nearly a packet and she'd had only a few, and she rested her case.

In 2010, Diana didn't smoke for four months while she was in hospital, not when she was allowed out on day release nor, towards the end of her time at the Lister, when I wheeled her outside for some fresh air. And for a while after she came home she still didn't smoke. The rest of the family tried not to smoke around her, but even when we went into the garden for a quiet puff she would observe us with the infuriating, self-satisfied disapproval of the reformed smoker.

But after a few weeks, when she felt mentally and physically able to write again, the nicotine craving returned. It was the same for both of us, a throwback to our early days in Fleet Street when nearly everyone smoked heavily and those who didn't were regarded as wimps. A good few years ago, during a summer holiday, Diana and I both gave up smoking for six weeks with the help of nicotine-enhanced chewing gum. But as soon as we had to sit down again in front of a word processor to start earning a crust, our hands automatically reached for tobacco and if it was not to be found our minds would seize up and we would be unable to write anything more than a few words. Yes, I know it sounds pathetic and it probably is, and reformed smokers and habitual non-smokers will doubtless sneer contemptuously. Well, sod them. That's the way it was and, for me, still is, and will probably continue until I gasp my last breath. It might be of passing interest, though, to the smug and self-righteous, that a few weeks before she died Diana had a chest X-ray and, after some sixty years of smoking, her lungs were completely clear.

Another thing . . .

When we were eating in a restaurant together and had ordered different dishes, she would stare at my plate and say, 'That looks good.' Then, unbidden, she would reach across and take a forkful of my food.

I would say: 'Look, if this is what you wanted, why didn't you order it?'

'Because I didn't know it would be so nice. You can have some of mine if you want.'

'I don't want any of yours. If I'd wanted what you're having I'd have said so. Just keep your hands off my meal.' But that never stopped her.

This really is a woman thing. Men don't do it. If a bloke goes to lunch with a mate and they order different items, neither would feel remotely entitled to reach out and scoff the other's grub. Women do it, though.

Lord, she could be exasperating, but then so could I. There must be numerous times in any lengthy marriage when one partner or the other wonders why he/she is putting up with it all and then pauses to ask: 'But what on earth would I do without him/her?' And if the answer is – as it was in my case and, I sincerely trust, in Diana's – 'I haven't the faintest idea,' you've got a strong and enviable relationship going on. Cherish it.

All I know is that I'd give anything to have her back nicking my cigarettes and food and infuriating the hell out of me. Because if I had that I would also have her companionship, her wit and humour, her wisdom, her friendship, her uncritical (in all important matters) support and, most of all, her love.

I really miss those things. And I guess I always will.

Acknowledgements

My grateful thanks to all who helped with the writing of the book, with particular reference to my agent, Gordon Wise, who suggested it in the first place, and the terrific team at Transworld – the boss, Bill Scott-Kerr, my hugely helpful editor, Michelle Signore, Kate Green, a terrier of a publicist, and Claire Ward, who designed the jacket.

Photo Acknowledgements

Index